IT IS
WHAT IT IS

Surviving Domestic Violence

KikiDee 'KiDe' Watson

British Library Cataloguing in Publication Data: A catalogue record for this book is available from the British Library.

ISBN: 9798544194934

Book cover design: Peaches Publications.

Editor: Lorenzo Allen

Typesetter: Winsome Duncan.

Proof-reader: Collen Doyle.

Contents

Special Dedication to My Dear Father

Saiz Monty Kwetemu
24/12/1952 – 01/01/2021
REST IN PEACE
"Will keep the fire burning".

ACKNOWLEDGEMENTS

First of all I would like to thank God who has been there for me throughout my journey. He has protected me, provided for me, and blessed me in many ways I cannot explain. I would like to thank Grace, Saiz, Scoutah, Trigger and Tait for being my family. I love you all.

My next thanks is to my Book Confidence Coach, Winsome Duncan, an amazing woman. I do not have words to express my gratitude. She gave me a chance at a time I myself had given up on me. I cannot thank her enough, but I know she will be blessed in abundance.

I would like to thank Lorenzo Allen for some wonderful editing and for engaging with me without judging me and of course I extent my gratitude to all the Peaches Publications team, for a fantastic cause. To Colleen Doyle, many thanks to you for brilliant proofreading, it was a nice finishing touch. Ruth Pearson, I would like to say thank you for walking me to the finishing line. You did a fantastic job, and it was a pleasure working with you.

Last but never least, My God, My Lord Almighty. You are amazing. You never seize to amaze me! Thank you for the most precious blessing…. my two beautiful girls.

PROLOGUE

Life is full of paths, different paths to guide us to our intended destiny. But what if the course we choose to follow, leads us to total confusion, a road with multiple lanes? We think we can trust our intuition; we think we know the right lane, but then, that leads us further off the path. We realise that we have reached the bottomless pit, cast with a dark shadow ready to consume us whole. Can we change the path while we still have time, or continue with the cycle? Breaking the cycle is not easy.

I was seduced by love. It gave me strength that surrounded my spirit with defensive walls, creating a barrier between me and the rest of the world. Nothing was going to stop me from indulging myself with this love that had taken me to new heights. This was the kind of love I had never experienced before, a kind that no other had shown me. It was ravishing and divine. My love was full of hope, faith, and dreams; my love endured all things. My love had no wrong and no faults. My love was perfect.

The bonds of love can be enchanting and seductive, but there can also be a dark side. I fell head over heels and completely gave into those emotions, but I was soon caught up in a violent tide. My emotions blinded me to the reality that surrounded me. Love used jealousy and obsession to lure me into a life of control and misery. By the time I realised what I had become, it was too late.

I had risen so high, that I could not see what lay below me. I could no longer reach the people closest to me. The light that once shone so brightly in my dream world had thrown a vast shadow, armed with a powerful, dark force. I entered into it intensively, so the deeper I penetrated, the harder it became to turn back. The love that once was euphoric and exhilarating, soon became love's most dangerous game. Love that once brightened my world and boosted my confidence leaving me feeling invincible, had cast a devouring shadow that drew me close to another level of danger. It took me on a one-way street; to a dead end.

My love came into my life in the form of a man, named Nikolas Martins. The intense emotions I experienced with Nikolas were immense and powerful. They made me self-assured and full of certainty, especially when no-one else had ever made me feel that way. He came into my life and managed to give me the jumpstart I needed to fill the emptiness in my life. I gave him all of my heart, trust, and loyalty, even my soul. In return, he gave me his undivided attention, and pleasure in ways I could not imagine. Sparks ignited and sparks flew from the intensity of our lovemaking.

As a result of my dysfunctional upbringing, troubled childhood, traumatic adulthood, and addictive personality, I left myself exposed and open to manipulation. When Nik came into my life, I was unsure who I was or where I was going. That, unfortunately, made me easy prey for a reign of control. His love sneaked up on me from behind and threatened to ruin me. By the time I realised the truth, I had gone in too deep. I got caught up by a wolf dressed in sheep's clothing who had endlessly professed his undying love for me, when all along he was enticing me into his sin.

My love for Nik, blinded me to his evil. My need for his affection ended up enticing me into a series of horrendous events. I was willing to give up anything to protect and defend him, I thought if I stuck by him, he would change and love me back. I thought that I would make him feel worthwhile by loving him, and then he might stop being so horrible and angry. They say the devil you know is better than the one you do not, it was true in my case. We had similarities in our background, both black sheep of the family, troubled by alcohol. The conversation was easy, and emotionally we were an instant match.

It was a confusing and painful situation which I would describe as, a relationship filled with alcohol, jealousy, obsession, and control. An affair in which love went horribly wrong. A fatal attraction. This is a tale of how two people, both in the grip of an addiction, got addicted to each other. It is about love that became dangerously violent; love that led to a fateful tragedy.

CHAPTER 1

It was New Year's Eve 2007. Our friends Silveria and Mendoza were throwing a party and my family was invited. Roderick, my then husband, informed me that would not be attending, so I made other arrangements with the children. My two girls and I were in town doing some last-minute shopping and decided to pass by my husband's office since it was on our way home. I found him with Mendoza's younger brother, Patrick, and his friend Harper, who were both trying to persuade him to go to the party to celebrate New Year's Eve with them, but Roderick stuck to his decision. He gave us money for a taxi and pizza, and I took the girls home.

We all dressed comfortably in our jammy onesies. I switched on the fire and ordered some pizza. We snuggled in front of the fire and watched TV waiting for our pizza delivery. I received a call from Roderick halfway through our meal, telling me to get the girls and myself ready, we were going to the party after all. I was confused because he had been so adamant from the moment we received the invitation, that we were not going. Now here he was, calling me out of the blue telling me to get ready for the party. Frankly, I did not understand why he did not want to go in the first place, Mendoza was like a brother to him, but I guessed and assumed Roderick may have had more dirty secrets he was afraid might be exposed. My assumptions only. At Mendoza's last party we had attended, I found out that my husband had another child. It was quite an eventful night, so I assumed he might have had more skeletons in his closet that some people knew about and I did not.

There was quite a big crowd, an array of food on the table and a fridge full of booze. The music was booming, and people were mingling. Silveria came to meet us and led us inside. Then Mendoza called me into the kitchen where he handed me a bottle of Teacher's whisky. It was a bottle especially reserved for Roderick and me, a very loyal gesture I thought admiringly, I felt important. I thanked him and took two glasses, a bottle of Coke and a bowl of ice and went to sit on the settee in the lounge where I poured a drink. There were other children there and they were all playing together except Angel who sat cuddled right next to me. Roderick, being a popular figure, was mixing with the people exchanging small talk. I made him a drink and took it to him in the dining room where he was seated with other guys at the table.

I had to pass through the kitchen to get to the dining room, Tuggy, Mendoza's right-hand man, was standing next to the fridge and was in charge of the alcohol. He was there with a few other guys, but one of them caught my eye, a tall handsome young man with long, neatly braided hair. Our eyes met, and we smiled at each other.

"Are you Tuggy's brother?" I asked. Everyone in the room burst into laughter. "What did I say?" I was baffled.

"Who do you think is better looking me, or him?" he asked with a cheeky smile on his face. "You are," I said with a big smile on my face. He looked so cute with his hair in single plaits framing his face and settling on his shoulders. He had a thick black moustache which was a perfect match for his pretty face. He complimented me on how well dressed and beautiful I looked. He was a very charming young man. He told me his name was Nikolas. I could tell he was trying to chat me up, so I told him that I came with my husband and children. He thought I was lying to get away from him, so I beckoned him to follow me.

"Come, I'll show you, my husband." I walked him to the dining room entrance and pointed at Roderick, who looked over me. I waved, and he waved back.

"So, you were telling the truth," he said as we turned back to the kitchen.

"I don't lie Nikolas," I told him. We chatted for a while longer, and he gave me a peck on the cheek showing his appreciation for a lovely chat. I went back to the lounge and saw Roderick sat on the settee next to Angel. He was pouring a drink; I joined him. I was having a great time, and so was everyone else. A few moments later, I saw Nikolas coming into the lounge. He sat on the arm of the sofa next to a girl, they were just beside the door. Our eyes met and we smiled and waved at each other, Roderick noticed. After a while, I stood up and excused myself to go to the bathroom, I stopped for a moment and spoke to Nikolas about how much we were enjoying the party. On my way back I did not see his foot in the doorway, so I accidentally tripped on it, and he quickly grabbed me to stop me from falling. We both laughed it off and I proceeded to sit down with Roderick again.

Roderick started going on about how Nikolas was after me and how I was encouraging him. I told him nothing was going on and that we just had an innocent conversation. I reminded him that I had pointed him out to Nikolas as my husband and would not have done so if there was more going on between us. Within an hour, I was told we were leaving the party because he did not like what was going on with 'the guy in braids'.

"You'd better be kidding me; you rang me after I had settled in with my children and asked me to get ready for the party and now you are telling me we are going home! We only just got here, it's not even midnight!" I yelled at him.

We had an argument about it, and I told him I was not his puppet that he could pull strings on and manoeuvre anyhow he wanted. I was frustrated and angry and had had enough, I was not taking any more crap from him. Mendoza, Silveria and Harper all tried to calm him down and convince him that he was reading too much into an innocent situation, but he would not listen. He was displaying some very bizarre behaviour which was insulting and demeaning to me. I refused to go home with him, I refused to be controlled, so I stayed behind with my children. He rang for a taxi and went home, alone. I knew I was in safe hands and a safe environment; Mendoza was like a brother to the family, and he and Silveria adored the children and understood Angel's needs.

Silveria suggested that I should spend the night there with the children and go home in the morning when the situation was calmer, I agreed. I went back to sit with my girls whilst Silveria prepared a room for us. I poured myself a drink and was enjoying the music and the atmosphere. Nikolas came to sit next to us, and I introduced him to my girls. He apologised for causing trouble between my husband and me, but I assured him that he had nothing to do with it. He took Star and sat her on his lap to cuddle her to sleep whilst I did the same with Angel. I took both girls upstairs to tuck them in then went downstairs to enjoy the rest of the party.

"Does your girlfriend not mind you sitting here with me whilst she sits there alone?" I asked, referring to the girl he had been sitting next to.

"Oh no that's not my girlfriend, she is my best mate's girl, he is somewhere in the crowd."

I sat with Nikolas the rest of the night and we shared the bottle of whisky that was meant for Roderick and me. We talked, drank, and laughed all night; he had a wicked sense of humour, and I had not laughed so loud in a long while. It was as if it were just the two of us in the room. We became so absorbed in each other and oblivious to everyone else around us. We totally blocked out our surroundings as we engaged in conversation and laughter.

It was soon time for him to go and he asked for my phone number, I told him it was not a good idea, so he offered me his number instead.

"Keep in touch so I can make you laugh some more," he said as he handed me the piece of paper, he had written his name and number on. I then proceeded to the bathroom and on my way out I bumped into Nikolas in the hallway on his way out. We said goodbye and hugged. It was not planned; it was a spur-of-the-moment thing. The moment our bodies touched something transpired. We both lifted our heads from each other's shoulders at the same time and our lips locked.

I quickly pulled away from him because I knew what I was doing was wrong. I was a married woman; even though my marriage was hitting the rocks, I was still Roderick's wife. When I looked in the kitchen, I noticed a guy standing near the door, he had witnessed the kiss.

"SHIT!" I said to myself and walked straight upstairs into the bedroom where my little girls lay peacefully. I slept on the single bed next to them and went home the following morning.

I did not see Nikolas again after that, although I would often think about him, and I imagined what would have happened if I had called him. I often thought of ringing him, but I was afraid, the thought of having an affair frightened me because the guilt would have killed me.

I bumped into him a few months after the party, when I was having a family lunch in Wetherspoons. Roderick had popped out briefly to buy some cigarettes. The children and I were seated at the table near the main entrance, and I stood up to get the girls some treats from the bar when I noticed him.

"Hi," we both said at the same time. Nikolas was trying to have a chat, but I knew Roderick would be back soon and did not want to risk it.

"I'm having a family lunch and my husband will be here any minute so I can't talk to you right now."

"How come you never called me?" he asked.

"Look you'd better go, I don't want any trouble." I turned away and proceeded to the bar
.
"Hey!" he shouted, "you look beautiful by the way."

I smiled as he walked away.

I could not stop smiling, he wore three quarter cargo pants and a white vest which revealed his fit and well-built broad shoulders. He had the physique of a rugby player. I later found out that was his sport during his school and college days. He looked really cute and I wished I had sat with him again so we could laugh like we had on our first night. It was from that day onwards that I started to think and fantasise about him.

One late night as I lay asleep in bed, I heard the front door bang shut and heavy footsteps coming upstairs. I saw Roderick enter the bedroom holding a bottle of whisky in one hand and a diluted drink in the other. He was in a state and I could tell something was wrong, so I pretended to sleep.

I watched him as he sat at the edge of the bed facing the mirror and staring hard into it, taking gulps from his drink. He was making unusual sounds and sighing a lot, so I knew something was definitely up.

"Hey!" he said in a stern voice whilst shaking me to get my attention. I made a groan noise as if I were disturbed from slumber.

"Wake up I need to talk to you!" He sounded furious. I opened my eyes and tried to speak but he cut me off before I could utter a word.

"Is it true that you kissed Nikolas at Mendoza's party the night I left you there?" He was not smiling. He looked fired up and I was scared.

"What? What are you talking about!?" My heart missed a beat. "*What the hell?*" I thought to myself.

"I asked you a question, did you kiss Nikolas at Mendoza's house?" he repeated.

"Why would you even ask me something like that? Of course not," I said to him trying to sound convincing. I looked at the clock and it had just gone after two-thirty am.

"Are you sure about that?" His voice was raised.

"Of course, I'm sure. Keep your voice down, you will wake the children," I said to him hoping to calm him down. Mendoza's party was over six months ago so I wondered who had waited that long to finally break the news to him. He was frightening me; I had never seen him so angry. He poured himself another drink.

"I was in the pub today and someone told me that you kissed Nikolas on the night I left you, the night you were flirting with him. Is that why you stayed behind?"

"Look Roderick, I don't want to argue with you, it is late at night and I have already told you that nothing happened I don't know what else you want me to say." By this time, I was out of bed and sitting next to him at the edge of the bed.

"So, you are telling me that if I phone Mendoza right now, he will tell me that nothing happened?"

"Don't you think if something had happened, he would have told you straight away when it happened? You consider him to be family, don't you?" I was trying to reason with him and calm him down at the same time.

"Okay let's go downstairs and call him now then," he said taking the lead.

"Now? Have you seen what time it is?"

"I don't care! I am going to find out the truth one way or the other!" I followed him downstairs my heart beating fast. I was praying inside that Mendoza did not implicate me or say anything suggestive. Fortunately, Mendoza managed to convince Roderick that he had not seen anything and that if someone had in fact witnessed the kiss, that person would have informed him, Mendoza, right away. He then told Roderick to calm down and ignore gossip because people were just stirring up trouble. Roderick trusted Mendoza and never thought his friend would cover for me, so that was the end of the confrontation although his behaviour remained bizarre for months to come.

I later found out that Noah, his younger brother, fed him the gossip. He happened to be hanging out with Nikolas and some other guys when one of them confronted him about the kiss without realising that Noah was Roderick's brother. But Noah did not say anything to his brother until Nikolas refused to buy him a drink at the pub that night. It made him mad, so he dropped the bombshell on his brother in front of Nikolas. Of course, Nikolas denied it and had begged Roderick not to start any trouble with me. But Roderick was already riled by this time. He felt betrayed and humiliated, so he wanted to square it out with me. "*That was a narrow escape*" I said to myself.

I began to think about Nikolas on most days and sometimes even imagined making love to him. I always imagined how it would be but was usure whether I would ever be able to be with another man after spending ten years with Roderick. It did not stop me from indulging my thoughts. My sex life with Roderick at that point was non-existent. I had stopped loving him and could not bear him touching me. It got worse as his mental health deteriorated.

Roderick left us in August of 2008. I was broken and devastated. I was lost for a while until I got the courage to get up and mend, because my children needed me. I approached the city council for support with housing. Because of our situation, we were considered vulnerable and therefore, were prioritised for housing. However, our property did not come through until September of 2009. We were put in temporary accommodation in the meantime, a three-bedroom house in Eyre's Monsell, with a back and front garden, which was good for the girls.

I was not alone, but I felt really lonely sometimes, and the wounds of Roderick's betrayal were still fresh. For several weeks I would often wake up in the middle of the night with his deceit on my mind; it all seemed unreal. I was in shock for an awfully long time and as the months passed, I got more frustrated and impatient.

The fact that I was speaking to my children and not getting anything in return was especially hard for me to take. Angel was six years old and still had major communication difficulties. She did not understand much and said nothing. She only made sounds when she was upset about something, or humming when she was happy. It bedevilled me to not know how she was feeling or what her thoughts were. Sometimes all that did not matter because she always appeared to be happy and comfortable. She was in a world of her own and would often wander off without warning. It happened twice when we were out shopping. She wandered off in the big Tesco inside the shopping mall.

I immediately alerted security, I was in tears because I often heard stories about children being abducted, and I feared the worst. I was incredibly lucky that she was found after a few minutes which seemed like hours to me. She had taken a wander to the Thomas the Tank Engine just outside. PHEW! I was always careful, it took only a few seconds with Angel, so I had to be more vigilant. Thank God I had managed to toilet train her again so that was one less worry, but everything in the house had to be locked away securely, including doors, cupboards, and drawers because of her lack of a sense of danger. We stayed at home most times in the garden or spent time across the road in the park.

Here and there, I would seek solace in alcohol. I would follow the routine with the girls as usual and after putting them to bed, open a bottle of wine and drown my sorrows. My daughter's condition pained me. The older she got, the more pronounced her condition became. I only wanted her to communicate and be able to express her feelings. It broke me sometimes when she got upset and I had to guess what was wrong with her because she was not able to tell me in words. All she did was repeat my words back to me. I could not wait to move into our new home. I wanted to decorate and use my creativity and produce a unique and cosy home for my children. I thought that would help me take my mind off Roderick. He had to disappear from my mind just like he had disappeared from my life.

One weekend I got so bored and lonely that I decided to visit Mendoza and Silveria, as she was off work for two weeks. Mendoza's children were also there so I thought it would be a good idea for the children to mingle and play. It turned out to be a good day, talking was helpful and I liked Silveria. She had always made me feel comfortable in her house. It was then that I learnt that Nikolas was in prison for fraud. He was serving an eighteen-month sentence.

Tuggy, Nikolas, and another guy had tried to cash in some dodgy cheques. He took the rap for the other two. I thought the fact that he was in prison would put me off, but it did not. In fact I wanted him more than ever. He was due out in a couple of months. The fact that he had made me laugh so hard on the first night we met, had made a huge impact on me.

~ ~ ~

I finally received the keys to our new house on a Friday morning at the end of August 2009 and planned to move in on Monday. I had so many ideas in my head and wanted to put them into practice. I took a taxi and went to view the property; I had seen the house before whilst the workers fitted the new kitchen, but I had not seen the finished product. It had two large bedrooms and a box room, a toilet, a bathroom upstairs and another toilet outside. The back garden was big and had a large shed in it. The garden needed a lot of attention; it looked like a jungle. It would take a lot of time and work, some bricks and stumps needed getting rid of. However, this made me really excited.

I went to Wilkinson's to buy some pink paint and all the tools I needed for painting. My goal was to decorate the girls' rooms before the weekend was over. I also ordered two beds and bedding to go with them. I had received back payments in child benefits so I could afford to get everything I needed, and the council also helped with a grand towards decorating the house. I decided that the girls and I would spend the weekend at our new house whilst I got to work. We went back to our temporary accommodation and picked up what we needed for the weekend. We passed through Argos and I bought two inflatable mattresses and a portable CD player because I knew Angel would want her music to replace her computer time.

I put up the beds and put all the toys in what was going to be my bedroom. There was enough space in the room for them to sleep and move around to play. I put my overalls on and got to work starting with the bigger room which I painted dark pink. I was excitedly anticipating the finished look when I heard a knock on the door. I went downstairs to answer it. Three young lads stood outside. They explained that they had seen that we were just moving in and wanted to see if I needed any work done. They had noticed the state of the front garden, I took them around the back and asked them if they could tackle the work. We agreed on a price and they began the difficult task as I went back to continue with my job.

I could see the guys working hard in the garden. I worked for two days straight with a few breaks here and there to chill with the children. By Sunday evening, I had completed both rooms. They looked smashing, and I was proud of my hard work, determination, and achievement. I had never painted anything before in my life, and I was amazed by the brilliant job I had carried out single handed. I painted the floorboards with a nice glossy white colour and the pink just threw itself over the room. The boys had also worked really hard in the garden it was hardly recognisable. The garden was bare except for a piled heap of rubbish which required a skip.

I asked them if they could meet me at the property the following day when we moved in to assist with moving furniture; they agreed, and I agreed to pay them extra. They kept their word and came the next day. They helped me stack all the furniture in the dining room leaving the lounge clear for decorating. I needed the house ready as soon as possible, so I contacted Mendoza to find some decorators. He sent his right-hand men, Tuggy and Shaki, who quoted me a price of £280.00 for the lounge, dining room and hallway. I intended to paint my own bedroom and bathroom.

The day the guys came to evaluate the property and work, they brought Nikolas with them. He was out on an electronic tag and was staying with Mendoza as he had registered that address as his release address. I spoke to him briefly because he had to rush for his curfew. He asked Tuggy for pen and paper before he left and jotted something down.

"There is my phone number; I am sorry it did not work out with your husband but if ever you need anything or just to talk, call me," he said, handing me the piece of paper.

"Actually, there is something you could help me with. I have two beds being delivered later on this afternoon; would you mind helping me assemble them?"

"Sure, my curfew is between ten a.m. and twelve pm and then again in the evening from six p.m. and eight p.m., so I could come later on today after eight," he responded. We agreed, and he left.

Tuggy and Shaki were still around when the beds came, so they helped me put them upstairs and left me a list of all equipment they needed for the upcoming job which was to start the following morning. After a Maryland take-away

I tucked the girls in and waited for Nikolas. The doorbell rang just after eight forty-five pm and I opened it. I was excited to see him; this time it was just the two of us, and we had never been alone together before. We gave each other a big cuddle and were both pleased to see each other.

"I can see prison has changed you, I mean physically," I commented.

"Really and how is that?"

"You look taller and broader."

"Well, it must be the prison food," he said jokingly and we both laughed into the kitchen.

"Look what I got for us..." I said as I pulled out a bottle of Teachers whisky from the cupboard. I took out some glasses and we went upstairs. From the day I met him at Mendoza's house, I never forgot him and now we were in a room together, alone. The three years did not seem to have affected on our connection because we spoke as if we were carrying on from where we left off. We drank, talked, laughed, and worked on the beds. I was having so much fun; his sense of humour was my main attraction, and I was laughing all night just like I had done when we first met. I was surprised at how at ease I felt in his presence. I was relaxed and was myself as if I had known him all my life. I was usually apprehensive with new people but with him even on the first day, I wore my own skin.

By the time we had finished making both beds, it was around four o'clock in the morning and we were both exhausted. The beds turned out to be more complicated than we had anticipated, especially the small princess bed. It was too late for him to go back, so we went downstairs to the dining room where the furniture was piled and squeezed onto the armchair. We continued to chat and shared a lot that night, including a long and passionate kiss. It felt good and this time we were not stealing the moment. We took our time to enjoy and appreciate each other. It was a beautiful romantic and productive night; we fell asleep in each other's arms.

He came back the same day after his ten to twelve curfew. We ordered pizza and sat down with the children and ate. It was a lovely feeling, a feeling I had not felt in years. We went to the park where we played and had fun. I loved the way he interacted with my children; it touched my heart. My girls liked him too, including Angel, who usually had difficulties connecting with people. After he left for his evening curfew, I played with the girls for a while and got them ready for bed. I watched them as they slept peacefully and beautifully in their new bedrooms in their own beds. I felt proud, happy, and satisfied. I went downstairs, opened a bottle of wine, sat down to reminisce. I had a big smile on my face. My heart felt light and I only had one person on my mind, Nikolas. Just then, there was a knock on the door, and that brought me back to reality.

I was not expecting him back, but there he was, standing in the doorway outside. I invited him in, and we proceeded to the dining room. I offered him a drink and we sat down, relaxed and chatted away and again we shared kisses and fell asleep on the same armchair. When he came back the following morning, he took us to a different park. We ran, wrestled, played football. He pushed the girls on the swings and helped them on the slide. He was hands-on with the girls and very energetic. Sometimes I would just sit back and relax and watch them play. I loved it, something I had always wanted from Roderick but never received. Quality family time; to engage with each other and value one another. I felt contented.

Since it was summer holidays, I became a bit reckless with my drinking and, I presume I felt a bit freer because there was an extra person to help me look after the children. When we bought food for our picnics, I always included a bottle of wine for myself and a bottle of cider for Nik. I was a bit taken aback by his choice of drink because it was the cheap cider that was usually associated with homeless people, but somehow, I shook it off. He was fun to be with, full of energy, helpful, made me laugh and treated my children well So to me that was all that mattered at that time. The Ace cider was a minor dent to his huge, magnificent character. From years of crying every day, I was laughing daily, for hours on end. It was brilliant.

The children's bedrooms were complete, and it was time to concentrate on my bedroom. Nik offered to help since I was doing it myself. As usual, after his evening curfew, he came over, and we got started. We worked hard and played hard. After the first wall was complete, we were both exhausted, so we sat on the air bed. During one of our absorbing moments, we got carried away and went all the way. We had sex, and I say 'sex' because it was over in a couple of minutes.

"I'm so sorry," Nik apologised as he pulled out of me rolling over.

"It's okay, I understand. You don't have to feel bad." I assured him.

"Shit!" we both said and laughed, making a big joke out of the whole situation.

"You've been locked up for a long time, so I get it, no need to apologise." We cuddled and fell asleep.

After he left the next morning, I felt disgusted, *"What have I done?"* I asked myself, full of shame and guilt. *"How could I be so careless and stupid?"* We had not used any protection; we got caught up in the moment and neither of us had brought it up. I was so scared of contracting HIV; I knew so many people that had died from the disease due to recklessness, and I had sworn that I would always protect myself. I was worried, so when Mendoza dropped off his workmen the following morning, I asked him to take me to the Royal Infirmary. I was going to get tested; my children needed me.

The sexual health nurses told me that I had to bring the other person involved for them to test me. It was an awkward situation for me but I had to talk to Nikolas for my own sanity. I was not expecting the reaction I received from him. He did not argue with me or ask any questions he simply said it was all right, just like that. The tests were done, and the results were due in three days. He told me how his father had died from AIDS and how much pain he had felt watching him suffer every day. It had affected him so much to see his dad waste away on his death-bed, that he swore to himself that he would die from anything else but AIDS. I bought some condoms on our way back because I knew it was just the beginning of things to come between Nik and me.

That night after the hospital visit, was the first time, we made love. I remember it like it was yesterday. We lay there just staring into each other's eyes without saying a word. For over twenty minutes there was silence. We communicated only with our eyes and our emotions. It was intense and electrifying. He was so beautiful to look at, I felt my heart melting.

"You are looking at me as if you are falling in love with me," he said to me softly, his eyes still interlocking with mine. I took a deep breath; something was happening to me for sure, but I was confused It was almost as if I could feel his soul. Our souls were communicating, saying pleasant words to each other using the language only spirits could understand. We both burned with desire for each other. By the time our bodies touched, the skies had opened, and there was no turning back. He scooped me into his arms and kissed me passionately. I felt his warm breath on my neck as he whispered in my ear. I experienced a strange sensation in the pit of my abdomen to the magical sound of his voice, so deep and full of command.

We kissed and caressed, searching each other's bodies. Our eyes penetrated each other; it was enchanting and the feeling so beautiful. Nothing else was on my mind except this man who was inflicting so much pleasure on my body, a feeling I had not experienced since Cuba. Moments later, I felt the weight of his body on top of me; every nerve in me tensed. I smothered a deep sigh as his head was buried between my breasts while his hands stroked my slender legs. His mouth catered for my erect nipples with a hungry searching sensation, sucking, and brushing them with his lips whilst holding them tenderly with his manly hands. I burned with desire and expectation. He kissed my stomach down to my abdomen, and soon his head was between my legs. My heart beating violently. A gasp of pleasure escaped my mouth. "Take me!" I cried.

With passion and tenderness, he raised his narrow hips and thrust into me; I gave out a soft moan. He was warm, hard, and delicious. I watched him as he plunged in and out of my body, I felt as though I might faint with pleasure. Our eyes never left each other. Our minds were lost. The only communication that was going on between us was that of body and soul. The kisses were long, passionate, and intense. Our breathing became heavier and the motion faster. His arms tightened around me and mine around him. I screamed out with pleasure as I burst, and he exploded inside me with a roar. We kissed and both knew that we had satisfied the sexual appetite we had for each other. It was magnificent. I had genuinely enjoyed our pleasurable lovemaking and that was the beginning of many more explosive moments to come.

CHAPTER 2

All work to the house was complete; themed with red, black, and white colours it looked cosy and fantastic. I was really satisfied with the end result, and I was proud of myself. The only job left was the garden. It had all been cleared I just needed a skip to dump the rubbish. I was too busy playing happy families with Nik and the girls for me to bother. I think it is fair to say that Nik and I were getting addicted to each other's company. The only time we were apart was when he was on his four-hour court ordered curfew and even some of those times were spent together. I cherished every moment we spent together, and he treated my children like his own. He was extremely good at dealing with both of them, despite their different needs.

I loved the way he was in love with me and the attention he paid to me. He was fun and eccentric at the same time, and we shared loads in common. When we were in the house, he would follow me everywhere. If I stood up from the sofa to go to another room, he was right behind me. He became fixated on me, and I found it intriguing. To tell the truth, I found it fascinating and adorable. It reminded me of when Angel was a baby and how she followed me everywhere, including the bathroom.

He enjoyed sleeping with me in his arms; the closeness we shared was so important to him. When I got up in the middle of the night to use the bathroom, he would follow. I did not know how it happened, but I was falling in love with Nikolas. He was four years my junior. When the whole thing started, I did not mean for it to go anywhere, I just needed a bit of company here and there and of course a bit of fun. After what happened with Roderick, I did not want to get close to another man, so I had made it clear to Nik from the beginning. But then the game was changing_, my emotions were getting involved.

Everyone around me warned me against Nikolas especially because he drank so much and had a care-free attitude. The Nik I knew, however, was kind, loving and caring. I loved everything about him; his physique, the way he looked and smiled at me and the way he spoke to me. He sent shock waves through my body each time I was with him. There was a deep meaning to how he looked at me especially when he made love to me, we were bound by the soul.

There was no point in pretending that there were no strings attached, we both had fallen for each other. Nik would walk miles just to come and see me. Whenever I called him, he dropped everything and came to me. I meant something to him, and I felt needed. That gave me a sense of belonging. We both needed each other and became dangerously dependent on each other emotionally. The word "no" did not exist in his vocabulary as far as I was concerned. He would do anything for me. The whole summer was spent with just the four of us, exploring different parks and attending different fun events like a proper family. I had never felt so happy. Nikolas was a lovely human being with a warm and kind heart except, like me, he had some demons lingering around him and because of that, the pair of us made a good recipe for a cocktail for disaster.

Soon summer holidays were over, and the children were back at school. Nik helped with the school runs and making breakfast for the girls. Star's nursery was two buses away, so he took it as his responsibility to drop her off and pick her up. He would make sure he was there to pick her up from home in the morning and was always on time picking her up from school to bring her home. It made such a huge difference in my life, especially given that Angel needed extra care.

One day he received a letter from the home office informing him that they had found him accommodation in a hostel in Birmingham. Before Roderick left, he had advised Nik to claim asylum, so he was still awaiting a response and had been offered NASS assistance. It meant he was not permitted to work, and he only received £35.00 a week for his upkeep. He had been separated from his wife and son, who lived in Derby, for almost four years. He was entitled to housing but at that moment he was basically homeless, I could not let him move in with me because that would have made our relationship official, and I was not ready for a full-blown relationship. Already the nights he was spending with me were becoming exhausting.

I knew I would miss him, but I also knew that I needed time to breathe_, the affair was going at full speed, and I felt a bit suffocated. It would have been fun if I did not have the children, but I had the girls to consider, and I needed to be responsible. Besides, I still had the garden to take care of and my bathroom to finish off. They had already sent him travel tickets for that Monday, so we decided to make the most of our last weekend together.

That weekend he asked me for some money, but I felt awkward about giving him any even though I could spare a few pounds. I knew he needed it for his new start, but I just felt uneasy. Next morning when I was making breakfast, I realised that I was out of milk and orange juice. I was in the middle of making breakfast and did not want to interrupt that, so I sent Nik to the shops giving him my bank card and pin. I instructed him to withdraw £10.00 from the machine and then buy what was needed.

"I want my receipt," I said to him before he left. He was back in no time; we all sat around the table and ate before going out for the day.

We had a lovely afternoon and I did my best to explain to the girls that they would not see Nik for a while. He played with them until it was bedtime and that night, I let him read their bedtime stories and tuck them in. He came back downstairs; I made some popcorn and we watched a movie.

"I am really going to miss you," he said as we cuddled cosily on the floor.

"Me too. I wish you didn't have to go," I replied as I rested my head on his chest. There was silence for a while then he put his hand on my face drawing it towards his. He looked at me right in my eyes, moments passed as our eyes locked. I could hear my heartbeat and my breathing, it felt as if he were sucking up all my energy because I was getting weaker and weaker. Something magical happened whenever our eyes were in a steady gaze, it was bewitching. His lips touched mine and planted a soft kiss. Then he pulled away and gazed into my eyes once again.

"I love you, Nicolette," he said. His words sent a beautiful sensation down my spine, I was getting heated up, and I wanted him. Our mouths touched, and our bodies locked in a passionate clinch. The bulge in his trousers told me he wanted me too. We kissed and fondled and slowly undressed each other. I sat on the floor naked whilst he knelt in front of me, also naked. I took him in my mouth with both my hands scooping his bum; he groaned with pleasure. We explored each other with our hands and tongues and lost ourselves in each other. The heavens opened up for us.

I moaned and groaned as he made sweet love to me with so much passion and intensity. He was selfless, always making sure he pleased me. He took his time to pleasure me, submitting to my wishes and ensuring it was pleasurable for me as much as it was for him. I was on cloud nine, I wished it could go on forever, I did not want to be anywhere else or with anyone else or do anything else. I wanted that moment to last forever. I loved making love to Nik; I enjoyed him by leaps and bounds and when we exploded in each other, it was like experiencing a humongous display of fireworks. I fell deeper and deeper in love with Nikolas each time he made love to me because it got better and sweeter each time.

When he left for Birmingham, I realised how exhausted I had been and how hectic the last couple of months had been. My body and mind were now getting the rest they had so desperately needed. My girls and I were back to our daily routine and I could focus more on our lives. Even though he was away, we spoke on the phone daily. There was a payphone inside the hostel he was staying at, and he waited for my call every day at eight-thirty pm, soon after I had put the children to bed, and we would talk for hours. I missed him terribly. He waited at the payphone, on time, every day without fail.

I decided to take my mind off him by concentrating on finishing off working on the house and I also started taking some driving lessons. I bought myself a second-hand white Toyota for £500.00 for extra practice. The day I was buying the car. Nik sent me a four-page-long text telling me what to look for and where to find faults in a car before buying it. Three hours later he was at my house, having managed to persuade a friend to drive him from Birmingham to Leicester just to make sure I did not get ripped off.

What a gesture, I thought to myself. Nik said he did not want anyone taking advantage of me. We phoned the seller to bring the car round which he had a look at and told me it was good enough for the price.

"Oh my God, you came all this way just to check this car for me?!"

"Yeah, cos you will be driving the girls, and I didn't want you buying a dangerous car or you throwing your money away on junk," he said.

"I am really touched, thank you," I said as I gave him a big hug. We kissed, and he said goodbye. It was a grand gesture in my eyes, no-one had ever done something like that for me before. My feelings grew even stronger but I never told him how I felt because I was trying to tell myself not to have any deep feelings for him. *Even though he is drinking excessively, he is making a responsible decision,* is what I told myself at that time and that was what I focused on.

After just a month in Birmingham he was transferred to Derby and this time he was moved into a shared house with one other person. Derby was good for him because that is where his son lived with his mother. He spoke so fondly of his son and always said he wished he could do more for him. He was often frustrated by the fact that he could no longer provide for his son. His ex-wife Anne-Marie had remarried, and Nik hated it that some other man was took care of his son. But being in Derby gave him a chance to spend more time with his son, Ted.

Derby is only thirty minutes away from Leicester on the train, so we saw each other every weekend. I explained that I could no longer see him during the week because it was becoming strenuous for me. He wanted my attention just as much as my children needed it and I was beginning to feel the weight of the whole situation. Also, I found myself drinking whenever he was around because he was always drinking. After my relationship with Roderick I swore to myself that I would never fall for a man who drank, but Nik drank just as much as Roderick. I realised after a while that he was in fact an alcoholic. If he did not have a drink, he would have the shakes, hot-and-cold flushes, and the sickness. It scared me a lot because I knew how it could end, having lived with an alcoholic for ten years. I watched Roderick go through the fits and I did not want to witness it again. The problem was that I was already attached to Nik, so for me to block reality, I also drank.

One morning as I was going through my post, I came across my bank statement. I noticed a withdrawal of £40.00 that was made on the day I sent Nik to the shops with my card. He withdrew the £10.00 I had asked for and got the receipt for it and then withdrew £40.00 and kept it for himself. I was startled. I tried to find other explanations but came up with none. It was all printed in ink right there in front of me; the man I was sleeping with and sharing my life with, the man I was falling in love with, had stolen from me. The man who was supposed to be my best mate. All this time we had been speaking on the phone he did not think to mention it.

I decided to confront him because I was feeling hurt and betrayed. His response was baffling; he did not attempt to deny it. He apologised saying that he had asked me for the money, and I had refused, but because he desperately needed it, he took a chance. He said that he did not tell me before because felt embarrassed that he had to stoop so low. We talked it over and I let him know how I felt; I told him that I was hurt by his deceit. However, he was my mate whom I loved. He had made a mistake and apologised for it, so I let it go. I respected him for not trying to deny it and for owning up straight away.

We continued seeing each other on weekends, he would jump the train at times as ticket inspectors did not operate on late trains, and other times I paid for his tickets. Financially things were getting a bit hefty for me, providing him with food, drink, cigarettes, and transport but at that time I did not mind. I enjoyed spending time with him, and my children adored him, besides, I understood the situation he was in. I was helping out a friend in need who was good company and a friend indeed. I also considered that for years my ex-husband had looked after me financially, so why not help someone else, someone I actually cared for?

Every Saturday, we still maintained our family day for quality time, I took the girls out, either shopping, to the cinema, swimming, a meal or just a walk or play in the park. Nik would come in the evening after my time with the girls, and that was a routine I never broke. On one particular weekend, Nik came to the house on a Friday afternoon; he said one of his friends had offered him a free ride, so he had decided to come a day earlier to save travel money. I had no problem with that, as long as he gave us our family time the following day.

After breakfast on Saturday morning, the girls and I went upstairs to get ready for our day out, Nik shouted from downstairs that he would do some checks on the car before we set off.

"Oh, how very thoughtful of you sweetheart, thank you" I shouted back.

"All set to go?" I said to the girls after a couple of hours of us getting ourselves washed and dressed. The house was eerily quiet, I shouted for Nik but there was no answer.

"He must be smoking in the garden" I said to myself, but he was not in the garden. *"Well, he must be listening to music in the car,"* I thought, so I opened the front door heading towards the parking space. The view was blocked by the thick green hedge, so I could not see clearly. When I got to the front gate, I noticed that the car was gone. *"Maybe he took it for a test drive,"* I told myself.

"C'mon girls let's wait for Nik and then we can go," I said as I walked back into the house. I phoned his mobile, but it went straight to voicemail. Half an hour later, I tried him again, and it went straight to voicemail; there was no sign of Nik or my car. The girls were waiting in anticipation, Angel became agitated, and started to hum to herself to calm herself down. I was getting agitated by the whole situation because I did not know what was going on.]

"Girls let's take a walk," I said to my babies trying to be as normal as possible not wanting to disappoint them on a much-anticipated day out, a significant weekly event and occurrence; routine. We walked to the shops taking the longest route in the hope that I might spot him, but to no avail. An hour had passed, and I could not reach him on his mobile, which was switched off. I had no idea of his whereabouts.

I was angry that he took my car without permission when he knew that I needed it to take the girls out. I also knew that he had been drinking and that he would be drinking and driving and to make matters worse, he did not have a valid driver's license nor insurance. As each hour passed my blood pressure was rising and was reaching boiling point. The more agitated I was, the angrier I became. I was fuelling up with anger, getting more enraged by the minute, I was fuming.

"Who the hell does he think he is taking my car and going off? What gives him the fucking right?" I was saying to myself pacing up and down the rooms in my home. I was anxious, agitated, and restless. My mind was going through all sorts of scenarios, not incredibly positive ones. I looked at my children and felt really bad for them; they had been all ready for a day out and yet nothing was happening, and they were too young and the situation too complex for them to even understand what was

happening. It took me a while to try and calm Angel down as she was anticipating her Saturday routine. I decided to distract them by putting some music on and dancing, it seemed to do the trick. I gave Angel full control of the remote and she became the DJ of the day whilst we waited for the drama of our car to unfold.

All the while, I kept looking at the clock. Five hours had passed, and still there was no word from Nik or about my car. I wanted to call the police to report my car stolen, but I did not want to involve the police believing they would start asking too many questions. So I ruled against it; my hands were tied. I ordered pizza for the girls and then took them upstairs for bed, I put DVDs on in both rooms, kissed them good night then went back downstairs to wait for Nik. I started drinking, and the more I drank the more agitated and enraged I became. My girls were tucked in and I knew they slept right through the night, so I waited like a hawk for a confrontation with Nik.

I was drinking because I was angry. I was drinking because I was frustrated. I was drinking because I let my girls down. I was drinking because, yet again, I had been betrayed by someone I trusted. I was drinking because I was worried about him.

On the one hand I was angry, but on the other I wondered whether he had been arrested and was in a police station somewhere or maybe he had been involved in a collision and was in the hospital. It did not matter because whatever was going on, the feeling of anger dominated my body and mind. The fact was that he took my car without permission and my children had been directly affected by his actions.

Around eight pm I had had enough of speculation, anger, and fear. It had been nine hours since Nik and my car went missing. I picked up the phone and rang the police. The phone was answered and just as I was about to speak, I heard my car pull up outside, so I hung up. By this time, the alcohol took its toll on my system, and I was seething with rage. I went to open the front door and waited. I saw Nik with his friend Mo; Nik was coming through the gate, drunk as a skunk. I grabbed the car keys from him and shouted all sorts of obscenities. He tried to enter the house, but I blocked him by pushing him away. Because he was so drunk, he lost his balance and fell backwards and landed on his back on the pebbles in the front yard.

Mo looked on from outside the gate, helpless and not wanting to involve himself in our business. Nik got back up on his feet and I pushed him back down. He asked for his jacket which he had left in the house, so he could leave. It was quite a chilly night, and he had to travel all the way back to Derby. I could not stand the sight of him at that moment. He had acted in a dastardly and selfishly which inconvenienced my children. There was no longer a place for him in my life. He had gotten away with stealing my money, but I was not going to let him get away with stealing my girls' quality time.

It was a very cold night, and all he had was a t-shirt and a pair of jeans, but I was reluctant to give him his jacket not after what he had put us through. He too had to be inconvenienced like we had been.

"Look, I need to get to Derby, and if I don't have my jacket I will freeze to death," he begged.

"Well, you should have thought about that before you stole my car innit!" I shouted.

"Okay, would it help if you spoke to my mum?" he asked as he reached for his phone from his trouser pocket. I had spoken to his mother a few times before, and she seemed a remarkable and reasonable woman.

"Hello, Ma….. Ma hold on," he said as he handed the phone over to me. I took the phone from his hand and I told her everything that had happened that day. I also told her about the incident where he took money from my bank account without my permission. She was not amused. After speaking to his mother, I handed him back his phone, slammed the door in his face and locked it. He was outside for a while shouting all sorts and kicking the door.

At that point, I was terrified because I had never seen that side of him before, it was a totally different Nik. The Nik I had known the past few months was gentle and kind and never had a negative word to say to me. What I was witnessing and hearing at that moment was mind-blowing.

The rampage went on for a few minutes, banging and shouting making noise for the neighbours and children. Suddenly, it went quiet; I heard the sound of the gate open and shut. I looked through the window and saw him walk away. What a relief it was. I settled down and had another drink, still traumatised by the events. It was a really terrible situation; I had lost my beautiful Nik. I did not recognise the barbarian that was at my door a few moments back. It was hard to take in.

The following morning, I saw a message waiting on my phone. It was from Nikolas. I got excited thinking he had sobered up and came to his senses and was apologising. I opened the text message and got the shock of my life, my heart collapsed.

> *"Hi bitch, I don't know who you think you are, but I want to tell you that you are a nobody. You are just a fat, and ugly, old woman, no wonder why your husband left you and was fucking prostitutes like Zarah. There is nothing special about you and if you think that I ever loved you then you are sadder than I thought. You are nothing but an old fucking sagging whore!"*

By the time I finished reading the message my face was wet with my tears. I was in disbelief. I thought my mind was playing tricks on me, so I read it again. It was the same text. My heart was pounding from pain and anger. I was in pain not only from his hurtful words but also the confirmation that Roderick was sleeping with that prostitute from his office. I could not breathe. Was this some kind of a sick joke? Did Nik actually say those things to me? My Nik? I thought there must have been a mix-up, that he was texting someone else and entered my name by mistake. I read the text over and over and each time I added salt to a fresh wound. I needed to speak to him.

"What do you want bitch?" is how he answered his mobile phone. He was incoherent and heavily intoxicated.

"The jacket you stole is not mine and I hope you are not planning on wearing it because you would have to explain to its owner how you obtained it. Fucking sorry arse-bitch!" and he hung up.

He sounded wasted; I had spoken to him when he was drunk before, but not like that. Even his voice sounded different. That was a switch from an angel to a devil at the flip of a coin, Nik was not just my lover; he was also my best friend. I felt soured by his betrayal. His words pierced through my heart, leaving an indelible mark. I had become attached to him and I thought we shared something tangible. I was not expecting a committed relationship, but I thought we were close. My children adored him, and he loved and cared for them. We had spent more than six months together with hardly any time apart and there was never a day that went by that we did not speak to each other, more than just once a day. I was going through another heartbreak; the pain was immense. Another debilitating rejection and loss.

Different negative thoughts were circling in my head. I felt like I was going insane. I cried for days and slept most afternoons when the girls were in school. Daily routines became difficult to tackle. I was struggling both physically and emotionally. Psychologically I was on the verge of a break down, so I went to the doctor's and was prescribed some anti-depressants. I tried the best I could for the girls, made sure they were well taken care of and did not let my low mood affect theirs. I had to be strong for them, I was all they had, and they were all I had.

During my school runs with Star, I met a mother whose little girl attended the same nursery. We would often meet at the bus stop and exchange conversation. We soon became friends and her daughter Marie -a year older than Star- soon became best friends with her. Nina was nine years my junior, but we hit it off right from the word go; she had a lovely personality. She was originally from Somalia.

I also had my friend Minty to talk to, whom I had met through my ex-husband who was friends with her ex-husband. We had known each other a couple of years; although we did not see each other often, she was always at the other end of the phone whenever I needed her, and it was the same for her. It was a pretty rough time for her as she was going through a divorce herself. It was a bad time for both of us and I was thankful to have her in my life. Her support made a difference, and soon Nina and I would also become remarkably close friends.

CHAPTER 3

I had to be strong for the girls, so I began working on the garden just to keep myself occupied and get Nik out of my head. I started by hiring a skip which was delivered within a few days. I worked on the garden everyday as soon as the girls were in school until the time they went to bed, taking breaks to drop them off, pick them up, wash them and feed them. It was a heavy job; there were a lot of boulders and heavy bricks, but I was determined to work hard, besides; I found it to be good therapy.

I was left with about two days' work and it was a weekend, so I decided to get some beers and worked through the last bit. After dinner that Friday, I opened a can of beer and went back to the garden to continue my work. Angel was on the computer in her bedroom and Star was in bed watching a movie. After an hour I went inside to check on them, both seemed content and settled so I let them be and went back outside. Another hour passed before I went inside for another check, Star had fallen asleep, so I switched her TV off, tucked her in and switched the lights off. I went into Angel's bedroom and it was empty. I called out her name but there was no show. Usually when I called out her name, she would come to me.

I looked in the bathroom, downstairs and upstairs again and there was no sign of her. I was in a real panic. My heart racing, I looked under the beds, behind the sofas in the cupboards everywhere even in some unrealistic places, I was desperate. It was clear that Angel was not in the house but where had she disappeared to? I realised the front door was unlocked, and ran frantically to knock next door. They had not seen her. I ran back to the house and phoned the police to report my daughter missing.

I feared the worst. Angel was severely autistic and did not have any speech, which made her extremely vulnerable. I broke down. Soon I had the whole neighbourhood searching for my daughter. All sorts of theories were going on in my head. I had never been so terrified in my life like I was in those moments. Everything seemed to be happening in slow motion. None of it seemed real and yet it was. It was so real: my little girl had gone missing and no one knew where she was.

> *"What if something horrible happens to her, like being hit by a car or meeting an evil person who will take advantage of her vulnerability. God, please protect her, help me find my baby, please God bring her back home safe and unharmed. God, please help me find her; I beg you."* I prayed.

As each minute passed my fears increased, I was paralytic, I did not know what to do, everyone else was out searching but I was told to stay at the house in case she turned up. I could literally hear the clock ticking, counting every second. I also noticed that her bike was missing which meant that she could have gone anywhere. I took out my rosary beads and sat on the stairs with the door wide open. I sobbed and started to pray.

"Hail Mary full of grace,
the Lord is with thee;
Blessed are thou among women
and blessed is the fruit of thy womb Jesus.
Holy Mary, Mother of God;
pray for us sinners
now and at the hour of our death.

Amen

Our Father, who Art in Heaven,
hallowed be Thy name,
Thy Kingdom come.
Thy will be done on earth,
as it is in Heaven.
Give us this day our daily bread.
and forgive us our trespasses,
as we forgive those who trespass against us.
Lead us not into temptation;
but deliver us from evil.
For Thine is the Kingdom,
the power, and the glory.
Forever and ever. Amen"

After what seemed to be a lifetime, I saw a police car pull up in front of the house. I ran outside not knowing what to expect. I saw one police officer coming out of the car, I could not read his facial expression because it was dark, and there was a crowd outside. Another police officer came out of the car and headed towards the boot. The first police officer opened the back door of the car and I heard him speak.

"C'mon," he said as he reached his hand inside. I saw the other police officer pull out a bike from the boot and at the same time, I saw Angel being helped out of the car.

"Oh my God!" I screamed as I ran to her. I knelt down and took her in my arms and held tight. I could hear voices around me, cheering and applauding. They had found my baby and brought her home safe and sound. She seemed oblivious to her surroundings, and must have been wondering what the fuss was all about. I thanked the officers and all the neighbours before taking my girl inside. Thank God that day after school I had dressed her in her t-shirt that read "**I am not naughty I have autism**" - which also had the National Autistic Society logo on it. When a member of the public saw her wandering the street pushing her bike, they tried to communicate with her and when she failed to respond they took her to the local police station where she had already been reported missing.

"Oh Angel, don't ever do that again. Mummy was terrified," I said to her. The sad thing about it all was that she did not seem to understand the situation. I was not reaching her and it broke my heart. I wanted her to understand that she could not just open the door and walk out because it was dangerous out there. We were truly fortunate that she came home safely. Part of her autism was unpredictable behaviour. My baby was growing up, and her mind was getting curious, so I knew I had to be more careful and more alert. I spent the night in her bed, holding her close to me, I guess it was a way of assuring myself that she was really home and that she would not get away again. I really thought I had lost her. It was a terrifying feeling indeed.

The following day was difficult for me, instead of focusing on the positive aspects, I concentrated on negative past events. The "what ifs". I had only a little bit left to do in the garden and I was hoping to finish by the end of that weekend. It would only take a couple of hours to finish so I got started on breakfast. I made sure I locked all the doors and removed the keys. I put the front door keys in my coat jacket that hung behind the door.

My work was done by lunchtime. My garden was finally clear and looking good, but I was exhausted. I prepared lunch for the girls and I went upstairs for a nice hot bath, which was much needed. I had planned on taking the girls to the fun fair later that afternoon. When I went downstairs, I was clean and refreshed. I went to get a can of beer from the fridge and sat down on the sofa to relax a bit. My body was still aching from carrying the heavy stones and bricks. Before I knew it, I dozed off.

"Miss Wallace?" I woke up to the sound of a male voice. When I opened my eyes, I saw a police officer standing over me in my lounge.

"Yes?" I responded in total confusion.

"We received a call from a member of the public about your children who were seen wandering across the main street. Are you aware that your children were out?"

"What!" I asked. I was perplexed. They explained how both girls were trying to cross over the busy street across from the house. I apologised to the officers and explained what was going on and about the incident the previous night. I also told them that I had ensured that I locked all the doors and hid the keys in my coat pocket.

"How many of those have you had?" he asked, pointing at the can of beer on the table. I told him it was the first one, and the reason I had dozed off was not that I was drunk, but was I simply exhausted from working in the garden. They must have been satisfied with my explanation because it was clear that I was not drunk. They then brought in the girls inside. The evidence of my hard work was just outside my gate in the skip.

One of the officers introduced himself as P.C Adams. He sat down next to me and spoke.

"Look I get how difficult it must be for you to bring up two girls single-handedly, especially given the extra needs of your eldest daughter. I am a family man myself and I understand. So, whenever you feel you want to talk to someone, here is my card, call me," he said as he handed me his card with his details on it.

I thanked both officers and they left. I shut the door and locked it and this time I put the keys in my bra. I considered that to be the best hiding place that she could not get to. Then I broke down. The situation was getting out of hand, I was losing control and I did not like that. I knew that as Angel got older, she would get harder to manage, but I never expected this. Star had just followed behind her sister. She was only three years old; anything could have happened.

I felt hopeless. The police now had two incidents on record, of my children going missing in a space of a few hours. It was their responsibility to inform social services. I was terrified I did not want to lose my children; they meant the world to me. To make matters worse, they had seen alcohol in the house and were aware that I had been drinking. I was too feeble to take the girls to the fun fair that afternoon as I had planned, so we stayed in and ordered a takeaway. I was in a paralysed state, and all I could see was darkness. I picked up the can from the table and finished its contents and there was more in the fridge. I drank because my mind was going insane. I drank because I felt hopeless and helpless. I drank because I was failing my children yet again. I drank because my children deserved better. I drank because I was losing control. I drank because I was in a lot of emotional pain. I drank because I did not know where to seek help.

Monday morning, I rang the head teacher at East Gate Special School, Angel's school. I informed her of the weekend events so that they were aware of Angel's behaviour and could be on the lookout. She was very understanding and supportive and advised me that I should not hesitate to contact her if ever I needed extra support. That week was a calm one, I locked the front and back doors and bought a padlock for the garden gate. I went to Wilkinson's for some gardening tools, some lawn seeds and manure. I spent the whole day with a digger and was done by the end of the day. The following day I layered the manure, spread my seeds, and watered.

Star had moved on from nursery to year one and so was in a different school, which was a ten-minute walk away. I became acquainted with one of her friend's mothers, whom I often bumped into during pick-ups and drop-offs. Her name was Joan and her daughter was Shelly. She also had an older boy who went to the same school. On Friday after school, she came with her children to my house wanting to borrow some money - said she needed £80.00. I did not have cash in the house and my computer had a virus, so I knocked on Angel's door and asked to use her computer to transfer funds into Joan's account.

Joan's children were fascinated by Angel's room, the flashing-coloured lights, colour-changing lamp, and the fake fish tank, and they burst in, entranced. This made Angel feel uneasy and she went to hide under the bed. I tried to convince her to come out, but she would not. It took me a few minutes to complete the online cash transaction and asked everyone to come out of Angel's room. When I looked under the bed, Angel was not there. We all looked through the entire house but did not find her. We looked in the garden, and she was not there either, we noticed that the front door was wide open.

"Oh no, Lord, not again!" I screamed. My eyes were off her for just a couple of minutes and no one had seen her sneak out of the room. There was panic everywhere. I was too scared to phone the police; another report to social services within ten days I could not risk.

Joan got into her car with her children, and I got into mine with Star and we went searching the neighbourhood. I left the door wide open in case Angel came back home. We met back at the house in ten minutes with negative results. We went again in different directions and searched. The time frame told us that she could not have gone far, but the results told us differently. As I pulled up in front of my house, I saw a police car and a police officer standing at my front gate. There had been sightings of a barefoot girl walking in the direction of Beaumont Leys shopping centre. As the officer was talking to me, a call came in through his radio. The same girl was now in Tesco at Beaumont Leys shopping centre, two-and-a-half miles away. She had gone to the delicatessen counter and when the caterers failed to engage her in communication, they called the police who were now with her.

They described the young girl and I confirmed that it sounded like my little girl. We were searching in the wrong places; she was headed in the opposite direction. She had to cross two busy main roads, including a roundabout. She had walked all the way to Tesco for their ready-made barbeque chicken! It was another shock to my system. I thought she might have gone to the local Co-Op, which was five minutes away, but oh no, it had to be that special Tesco chicken. She was becoming bolder and more adventurous. After a few minutes, another police car pulled up and handed me, my baby. What a relief of despair. The record was not looking good but at least this time there was no alcohol involved. Nevertheless, it was not looking bright for me with social services.

I explained to the officers how she had managed to sneak out, I was shattered. It was third time lucky that she ended up home safe and unharmed, but what if it happened again and we were not so lucky? What frustrated me the most was that I had managed to gain control of the situation, but because I let people into my house, I slipped up and disaster struck. I was so angry with myself for letting the kids go into Angel's bedroom and disturbing her space. My thoughts were filled with "if only".

If only Joan had not come to the house. If only I had made sure that I locked the door behind them. If only I had not allowed the kids to enter Angel's bedroom. If only... The guilt and frustration overtook me, it was overwhelming. I wanted to do my best to protect my children, but I seemed to be failing them. My mind was so convinced that social services were coming to take my babies away from me. My mind was certain that I had reached the end of the road. My mind convinced me that I had slipped up big time and that I would to lose it all.

I put the girls upstairs early that evening and put DVDs on for them, I struggled to focus on solutions. Instead, I was focusing on the past, the difficult journey that had been filled with pricking thorns and stumbling stones. A life journey filled with blood, sweat and tears. Filled with regret, lament and never-ending heartbreaks. What was the real purpose of my existence? I wondered to myself. From the day I was born, I knew nothing but suffering and sadness. I knew neither love nor laughter; nor how it felt to belong. Heartache and tears were all I knew; in fact, they had become so normal that each time I felt happy about something, I would feel bad because I knew the pain was lingering about. Each time I had a happy moment something terrible would happen afterwards that made me sad. My heart filled with fear and guilt, followed by restlessness and palpitations.

I could not sleep that night; I had a bottle of wine and a few cans of beer. Instead of blocking out the bad memories and numbing the pain. I was opening up a lifetime of horrors and nightmares. It was like watching a movie of my life playing back from childhood with every experience, every person, every thought, and every word that had left a scar in my heart.

The following morning after breakfast I drove to Nina's house and told her what had happened and that I felt low. I asked her to watch Star for me while I spent some quality time with Angel. I thought she might need one-on-one attention which she never had with me since Star was born, after five years of just me and her. I told her that I would pick Star up later that evening or the following morning. Star was more than happy to spend the night at Nina's house, she missed her friend Marie since they were now both attending different schools.

Angel and I had the whole day to ourselves. She had my attention all to herself. We drove around for a while listening to music in the car. We went to the park, played on the swings and slide and then went to Tesco to get her favourite chicken. We arrived home and we ate and she stayed downstairs with me the whole time. We played musical games and building blocks and she engaged really well. It was a special day, much-needed quality time. I could tell she was happy, especially when we discovered something in the garden. It was all covered in green; the lawn had shot out. It looked so beautiful; a magical moment.

"Look Angel, grass" I said to her touching the lawn. She gave me a huge smile of approval. I took out the Argos catalogue and we sat down looking at garden toys while I made her point to what she liked. After a while, she retreated to her bedroom and went on her computer. Whilst she was upstairs, I remained downstairs with my thoughts and a bottle of whiskey which I was diluting with strawberry milkshake. The more I drank, the more I sank into depression. The more I looked around the house the more it reminded me of past events. I was driving myself crazy, and I needed to escape.

"Angel", I called out. As she came downstairs, I handed her a coat then put mine on and picked up the car keys. Without thinking, I poured myself another drink before heading for the car. I sat Angel in the back seat, buckled her up and took the wheel. I was not thinking of the consequences I was focusing on escape, but I was escaping using a very hazardous route.

"Let's go for a ride" I said as I turned around to look at her. She wore a big smile on her face; she enjoyed going for a drive. I was drunk and I was not thinking straight but I felt much calmer than I was before. I drove around for three hours and drinking without reflecting on the possible consequences. It was not a busy time of day and I was driving around the neighbourhood going nowhere in particular.

My mistake came when I decided to drive into town. It was a Thursday, which was a students' night, so it was terribly busy; but I did not know that at the time. I was driving around in no particular direction, then I entered a street lined with nightclubs. That was where all the action was happening. I was fascinated by the vast number of people all dressed up on a night out. My mind got so involved with what was happening outside, and before I knew it, I had hit two bollards and three parked cars. I felt the air cushion blown in my face and heard Angel humming. The car was filled with the smell of fumes and I checked to see if Angel was all right.

I got out of the car and pulled her out. People were already gathering at the scene. I was in a state of shock. I held on to Angel so tight and reached for my drink in the car, mixed in a carton of milk. I took a long swig. All I could hear were loud voices. I was frightened and, in a trance, I kept drinking. I stood there in a frozen state not knowing what to anticipate. I was still holding on tight to Angel, I was horrified.

A few moments later, the ambulance and police turned up. The police asked me to walk with them to their van. One police officer tried to take Angel from me, but I refused to let her go. Another police officer tried to force me to let go but I resisted.

"Don't touch her!" I shouted. "Please don't take her away," I cried. I was handcuffed and shoved in the back of the van. I prayed the whole way loudly, reciting my Hail Mary prayer. At the police station, I refused to co-operate with the officers. I was on a rampage and it took six police officers to hold me down and restrain me. They wanted to know where Star was, but I refused to tell them. They locked me up in a cell and I knew then, that I was in deep trouble.

The next morning, they informed me that they had managed to locate Star at Nina's house after knocking on a few doors. They took Angel to Nina as well, and that was where she was being looked after. It was such a relief for me, I could not have asked for a better person to look after Angel. On my first offence two years back, I had been charged with 'being drunk and disorderly whilst caring for a child under seven years old and assaulting a police officer.' This time I was charged with 'driving with a minor in the car while under the influence of alcohol.' I was released the following day on bail waiting to go to court.

The days that followed were gloomy days for me. I did not know what was going to happen to me. I could be facing a prison sentence. If so, what would happen to my children? My thoughts were making me insane, and the fear was getting in the way of my daily routine. My mind became my own enemy; my mental prison. Eventually, the time came, and I was given an eighteen-month suspended prison sentence and 150 hours of unpaid community work.

~ ~ ~

For a while, life was normal. I was managing the household and the children's lives well. I had installed alarms for both back and front doors and all the windows. I had a lock and key for the garden gate, and I kept a close eye on Angel. Our garden was impressive, twelve-foot trampoline, three seat swings, a slide, a three-seater swinging garden chair, a hammock, inflatable swimming pool - not to mention the table, and six chairs and a barbeque. We called it our "mini-park" All the kids we knew loved coming round to play. It was such a joy to lie on my hammock and watch the girls play and have a good time, *"I did this,"* I would always tell myself. When my insurance money came through, I bought us a red BMW car.

Beautiful car, beautiful house, beautiful children, life was beautiful, it was good_, in fact it was too good to be true. It frightened me. Good things did not happen to me. I was so afraid that it was all going to be taken away from me. It scared me more than anything. Amid the laughter and the smiles, there was always fear lingering at the back of my head. I was comfortable and happy. That was not normal for me, so instead of enjoying what I had, I dwelt on the fear inside me which was greater than anything else I felt.

We had a routine which worked, and it made our life simple and enjoyable. At weekends we had Nina and Marie over for a sleepover, they would come Friday after school and we would all have dinner together before they left on Sunday afternoon. The girls were close too. She became close too, she became like a little sister to me. She was the only person I felt safe to leave my children with, especially Angel. I trusted her with my emotions and experiences, and I was comfortable talking to her about anything. Minty and I remained in touch. She had known me longer than Nina, and knew about my life of being married to Roderick, and I also knew about her marriage to Zex.

CHAPTER 4

Leicester Carnival 2010

The children were excited; I was excited. We were all looking forward to the carnival. I put on my jacket top and matching leggings, with army print and zips. I wanted to look nice, so I put some effort into making sure that I did. Both girls' hair was braided in long extensions. Both wore denim boots and denim shorts with summer tops. They looked gorgeous. Minty, Nina, Marie, my girls, and I were all going together. The children went in Minty's car, and I drove with Nina. It was such a beautiful day, and we were all in the mood for having fun. As I was looking for a parking space, I spotted Nikolas crossing the road with a couple of other guys. My heart jumped.

I had not seen or heard from him in four months and part of me knew that he would be at the carnival and maybe that was the why I had put so much effort into my physical appearance. I had removed him from my head because of the hurt he had caused me. He had a big impact on my life, even though we were together only for a few months. I was not sure how to react but one thing I was sure of was that I wanted him to see how good I looked. I decided I was not going to talk to him. He was with his friend, Marnie.

We were having fun walking around seeing different exhibitions and enjoying the rides. We bumped into Marnie and Nikolas, and I only greeted Marnie. Everybody else exchanged pleasantries with each other. Nikolas and I looked at each other and did not exchange a word, then we parted ways.

"Toilet," Angel said to me as she signed, "toilet".

"Guys, I need to take Angel to the toilet, where shall I find you?"

"We will be at the barbeque stand," replied Minty.

"Okay, won't be long. C'mon Angel, let's go toilet," I said to her as I reached out my hand to take hers. There was a queue at the toilets, and when our turn finally came, I put Angel in one cubicle, and I went into the next. I explained to her that she needed to wait for Mummy and not to leave. Whilst I was in the toilet, I kept calling out her name just to assure her that I was still inside and for her to wait.

When I came out of my cubicle, I did not see her, I tried calling out her name expecting a sound or reaction, but it was all in vain. The door where Angel had been opened, but it was a different person came out. Angel was gone! I was in a panic and became frantic. I ran outside and looked around; she was nowhere to be seen. I asked people around if they had seen her, but no one had. I walked back the way we came thinking she had gone back to the spot we were at before. I became hysterical.

Carnival was a big event with hundreds of people attending and loads of different activities going on. If I had lost her, if she had wandered about, how was I going to find her?

> *"Please, Lord, not this again. I came here to have a nice family day out, why is this happening? Am I not allowed to have a normal happy life? Should I have stayed home and been miserable? Please Father, help me find my baby before we have to involve the police. I beg you Lord, please help me find her. I beg you."*

"Angel's gone missing!" I cried out when I got to Minty and Nina.

"What?!" they both cried out. We started searching frantically for Angel.

"Look Mama Angel, I know you said you want nothing to do with Nikolas but right now we need as many people as we can to search for Angel." That was Minty talking reason to me. As soon as we told him, he and Marnie joined the party in the search for Angel. I was in tears and feared for the worst, but I tried to stay calm. I was dreading a potential disaster ahead of me.

We set a meeting point, where Minty stayed with the children whilst Nina, Nikolas, Marnie and two others split up for the search. The more we searched and could not find her, the more scared I became. I looked around her favourite rides, the trampoline, the music stand, but did not find her, my heart was breaking. I turned back and headed towards the meeting point, I met Nina also on her way back, and we both shook our heads. I was in a state and then suddenly,

"Mama Angel, look, there they are!" Minty screamed and pointed. It was Nikolas holding Angel's hand and Marnie walking just behind them. I ran and took hold of my baby and sobbed.

"Angel you need to stop doing this to Mummy. I was so scared. I told you to wait for Mummy. Oh, baby girl, what am I going to do with you? I love you so much." I squeezed her real hard in my arms like I never wanted to let her go. I looked up in the sky, *"Thank you, Lord, thank you for bringing her back safely, again"*

"Where did you find her?" I asked Nik.

After all that I was really grateful to him, I gave him a big cuddle, which ended up in a kiss. It was an exceedingly long and passionate kiss. From that point we sort of hung together at the barbeque stand where they were also playing music and a lot of people were mingling. Angel was under my grip and was going nowhere.

Later, a few feet from where I was standing, I saw Nik chatting up a girl, "Guys watch this." I said to Marnie, as I put Angel's hand into his and walked towards Nik and the girl. I stood right in between them and planted a kiss on his mouth. He responded. We kissed and never even realised that the girl had walked away. I looked back to Marnie,

Nina and Minty and gave them thumbs-up. I had no idea why I did that. I guess I wanted to prove to myself that he still wanted me; that he still could not resist me. I had achieved it gave me such a boost and a lot of satisfaction. I had enjoyed toying with him. It was my way of getting back control and staying in control. His text message had destroyed a part of me, and I wanted it mended.

Minty and I made plans to go out that night, so Nina was going to look after the children, they were all going to sleep at her house. Marnie, Nik, Minty and I had a few drinks at my house before we ditched the boys and made it a girls' night out.

When I go out, I get really wild; I lose control and enter into this crazy world of fantasy. The alcohol, the loud music, the crowd, and the indistinct loud voices become overwhelming, I get excited beyond imaginations. There is a person inside me that comes out that I do not recognise, and that person scares me. I get overexcited and feel as if I am in a different world where there are no rules or regulations. A world that allows me to let the steam out without thought or reason. That world has no limits to what I do, say, drink or smoke. And definitely no thoughts of consequences.

Nik was still living in Derby, but after the carnival, he remained in Leicester until he got me back into his life. Four days after the carnival, I finally gave in; he came over after I had put the children to bed. The sex was amazing, right there in the living room, the passion was breathtaking. We had spent four months without each other, and that day proved how much we had missed each other and how much we were pining for one another. It was mind-blowing. From that moment on-wards our lives began to create great waves and infernos.

I did not want to be honest with myself, but the truth was, I had fallen in love with Nik again and I was not about to let go despite his weaknesses. I was determined to help him through his alcoholism having lived with an alcoholic previously. I honestly believed I had the power to change him. When I first got involved with Nik it was so beautiful, especially when he followed me around like a little puppy.

He was obsessed with me and I was fascinated by his obsession; in fact, I think we were both obsessed with each other. There was so much passion between us, it scared me. I fell in love with him despite what people said, I knew deep down that I was living dangerously by carrying on with Nik. At first it was for company and sex, then feelings began to take over. We enjoyed each other's company so much we spent more and more time together. At times he would stay with us for two to three weeks at a time - especially during the long school holidays. But soon the relationship took a twisted turn.

"Can you be my girlfriend?" he asked me one day. I turned him down because I saw no future with him, I did not see him as boyfriend or husband material. He did not seem to care much about life. Always joking about how he was going to die at thirty-six years old. He seemed so sure and kept repeating it on different occasions.

"Nicolette, you are going to be the death of me. Someone told me years ago that I would be killed by the person I fall in love with. I have fallen deeply in love with you. I have never felt like this with anyone, so I am afraid that *you* are going to be the death of me."

It was all nonsense to me, so I stopped listening, but his behaviour made me doubt myself. One day during another one of our passionate lovemaking, I gave in.

"Yes, yes, I will be your girlfriend," I said. Boy had I fallen deep for him. The sex was magical, he knew me and understood my needs. He explored each and every part of my body carefully and systematically. It blew my mind.

"I love you Nico," he whispered in my ear with a voice full of intense desire.

"I love you too Nikolas Martins," I responded.

After picking Star up from school one afternoon, I heard her call him *dad. "Dad?* Did you tell her to call you that?" I quizzed.

"No, even I was shocked when she called me that. Shelly ran to me when she saw me at the gate, then Star ran too and held on to me and said to her. 'He is *my* dad'. "It sounded like she was warning her off," he said, jokingly and we both laughed.

I had observed the behaviour myself on the days we picked her up together. She did not want Shelly running for Nik so she would overtake her, and you could see she was competing for attention. From that day onwards it was "Dad". I did not try to correct her because he was the only father figure she knew. He had been in her life since she was three years old. He was the one who picked her up and dropped her off at school. I thought to myself that if she could feel so comfortable to call him that, then he must have been doing something right despite his alcoholism. He did a lot with the girls. He cooked for them, took them to the park and played with them in the garden. He was involved like a real father would be. In fact, he did more than Roderick ever did with the children.

There was an incident when I wanted to get something from the shops, so we all got into the car and Nik was driving. The shops were only two minutes away, but I did not feel like walking. Just as he was parking in front of the shops, there was a police siren behind us. They stopped and walked to our car. They asked Nik to go with them to their car, suspecting that he had been drinking and driving. Star broke down, wanting Dad back. She cried so hard that I had to go and find out what was happening. They told me they were arresting him for drunk driving. I explained it to her that Dad was going away for a little while but would be back. I watched my baby weep as they took Nik away.

"Can I go with him?" she asked, clearly broken with tears pouring down her face.

"No sweetheart, children are not allowed where they are taking him, but he will be back soon I promise. They just want to ask him a few questions, that's all. Don't worry we will wait for him together at the house okay?" I tried to console her. Angel was just humming a tune to comfort herself and kept repeating his name.

That is when I knew how much they cared for him and how much he meant to them. When we arrived home, I could not get Star to settle, so I inflated a mattress downstairs and assured her that when Dad came home, we would be waiting for him, and that seemed to do the trick. Although Angel could not speak, I could tell they had created a bond because she actually went to him sometimes to ask for help, something she usually did only with me.

Even though I knew there was no future in our relationship, I still went along with it. I lived and enjoyed the moments. Sometimes we would have Marnie and his wife Lisa, over or we would go to their house, Marnie was one of Nik's closest friends. The other friend he introduced me to, was Leo and his wife, Marcy. They also came around to ours, or we would go to their house. Every one of us was a drinker except for Marcy, so whenever we got together, we were sure to be drinking.

Marnie and Lisa had a baby boy, Jay, whom we went to see in the hospital when he was born and Leo and Marcy had a baby girl, Rose, who was a year old when I met them. Leo had other children from two different women who were older than Rose and he had contact with both of them. As I got to know them, I realised that Leo was a philanderer, he chatted up any female that passed him. But one thing I knew for sure was that he took good care of his wife and children. He loved Marcy, but that did not stop him from straying. Leo owned a navy-blue BMW and Marnie owned a silver Mercedes Benz; I had a red BMW coupe, and the three cars often went in convoy on days out.

One day there was a knock at the door and I went to answer it. Nik had just popped out to the shops. In front of me stood Leo and a woman I had not seen before. She was holding a baby. I invited them in, and we sat in the lounge. He introduced his lady friend to me as Kimberley. She lived only a few blocks from my house, but I had never met her. She was one of Leo's many 'girlfriends. I asked if I could speak to Leo in private and we went outside in the garden. "Leo, I don't like this. I cannot be entertaining one of your lady friends in my house, what would Marcy think of me if she found out?"

"N, you know my wife doesn't leave the house and doesn't mix with people, so she will never find out unless you tell her, which I don't think you would. Would you? C'mon N, it's just a bit of fun loosen up," he said.

"No Leo, it's not just about Marcy finding out, it's about morals. I feel like I am betraying her."

"You haven't even known her that long, I'm your mate, c'mon Nico." He was still trying to convince me. Just then the door opened, and it was Nik back from the shops. They greeted each other and asked what we were talking about, noting that we had left Kimberley all by herself in the lounge. I explained to him what was going on and they both told me to chill.

"So, Nik can bring a girl to your house and you will entertain her, is that what you are saying?"

"No," they both answered.

"No, you know Nik adores you and besides, his mistress is cider, he has no room for any other." Leo went on to say, jokingly and we all laughed.

"Sweetheart, I am always with you, so where do you think I could get the time for an affair?" Nik said. We all went inside, and Leo excused himself saying he was going to get something from his car. Apparently, Nik and Kimberley already knew each other, she was one of Leo's regulars. He had been to her house several times before with Leo, even though she lived with her boyfriend. Leo came in with a crate of Budweiser beer for him and Kimberley, a three-litre bottle of White Ace cider for Nik and a bottle of Blossom Hill soft and fruity red wine for me. We spent the whole day together in the garden drinking, chatting, and watching the girls play.

It soon became a regular event; we hung out more with Kimberley and Leo than we did with Marcy and Leo. Because Kimberley was a drinker like me, we hit it off right away. We would either hang out at my house, Leo's house, or Kimberley's apartment. Apparently, Leo had introduced Kimberley to Marcy as a friend so most times the five of us would hang out together with Marcy not having a clue as to what was going on. At times it would be the six of us including Thomas, Kimberley's boyfriend, who also had no clue about the affair. Marcy and Thomas; the only two people oblivious to the immorality around them. With time, I let it go, and it became a normal situation. After all, it was not my business to concern myself with their problems. Occasionally, we would hang out with Marnie and Lisa or just Marnie.

Life was good. Nik was loving and attentive. He would walk miles just to come and see me. Whenever I needed him, he was there on time and not a minute later. It did not matter where he was, who he was with or what he was doing; if I needed him, he was there without fail. He introduced the girls and me to his son and told his son that Star and Angel were the boy's sisters and to treat them as such and look out for them. He also introduced me to his ex-wife Ann-Marie who was then pregnant from her second husband when I first met her. We all had a good and civil relationship. We would drive up to Derby to pick up Ted and spent the day with him before driving back to Leicester. The children got along really well, and Ted was always on the lookout for Angel. Nik and I had explained Angel's condition to him, and he understood her pretty well. Ann-Marie and I would speak on the phone occasionally when we were arranging contact. She was pleasant and we respected each other in every way.

Nik always told me how much he loved me. He often uttered those three little words (that had never been spoken to me by my ex-love of my life, Cuba, nor by my ex-husband, Roderick) _ "I love you", always assuring me. I loved hearing him say it especially without prompting, and in time I learned to say, "I love you too." It took me a long time because I could not believe that someone could actually love me. I always believed that I was unlovable and so I used to get angry with him for saying it because they were meaningless words to me.

We did crazy and exciting stuff together. For instance, I remember one night when he asked me to put my police uniform on. He loved it when I dressed up. I had all sorts of outfits for our role playing during sex. I wore the full kit and had my handcuffs and baton in my hand. It was a sexy short dress which I wore with silky black tights and high-heeled boots - not forgetting my cap. I looked at myself in the mirror. I looked hot. I wore my makeup and everything and then made my way downstairs. The look on his face said it all. He got up and went upstairs. Seconds later he was holding a blanket in his hands and he took the car keys from the table.

"Let's go," he said taking me by the hand and walking towards the door.

"Go where?" I asked in confusion. I looked at the time and it had gone just after two in the morning.

"It's the middle of the night what about the children?" I quizzed.

"Don't worry, I have already checked on them and they are both fast asleep. We're not going far, c'mon _," he said as he opened the front door still holding my hand. We got into the car and after a few metres he stopped and parked. He opened his door and came around to open mine and again took me by the hand. He led me to the park across the road; it was a huge park, and it was deserted. After walking right to the middle of the field, he spread the blanket on the grass. And there, right in the middle of the park, he made sweet love to me, it was the most beautiful and romantic gesture. And just as we reached climax it started to drizzle.

"See even God himself is giving us His blessings," he said as he lay on top of me, still inside me. I looked at him in the night light. He was the most handsome person I had ever laid my eyes on. He looked so beautiful and majestic under the moonlight and the shining stars; he made me feel beautiful and special. That was one of many of our wild rendezvous. We made love in a tree once in the middle of the day with only the cover of the leaves to shield us from the public eye. It was enjoyable for me but hard work for him because he had to make sure we did not fall off. We made love in an abandoned flat where there was a police caution saying, "Do not cross". It was fun and thrilling and we loved doing it together.

Even though Nik could not support me or contribute financially, he was there for me in many other ways. He was there in the areas that needed tending to; my emotions, my passions, my fantasies, and my thrills. He fulfilled them all. He brought laughter into my life, gave joy to my children and we all shared some of the best moments of our lives. He became a significant figure to us.

Whatever Nik and I lacked in each of our lives, we found it in each other. We became emotionally dependent on each other. It was toxic and yet we carried on indulging each other with the poison of our passion. We were both drinking from the poisoned chalice and soon the full effects would be felt, followed by the many innocent casualties.

~ ~ ~

Things began to change when Nik started breaking the rule of, '**we see each other ONLY on weekends.** I needed the week to concentrate on my girls, give them all I had, focus on their well-being, education, and development. Monday night through to Thursday night were set aside for me. My time, my space, and my thoughts I needed those three to stay focused and sane. He started by leaving the house early Monday morning before the girls woke. The previous night would have started with him wanting us to be intimate after putting the girls to bed, the time that he should have been leaving. I could not resist him, and those feelings blocked my mental capacity completely. I did not think of anything else but the wonderful sensation he was giving me. He would make love to me till the early hours of the morning when transport was no longer in operation.

It started to happen often, and I did not like it one bit; it was disrupting my Sunday night's rest and sleep in preparation for the week ahead. And yet I could not stop it. I wanted him each time. Monday mornings became Tuesday then Wednesday morning. I was becoming exhausted because of the added pressure of attending to Nik. It was beginning to affect me in a negative way, but I could not get myself to tell him. It affected me to the point where I would not speak to him and he would ask me several times if I was okay. I always told him I was fine even though I was dying inside. He was disrupting my routine, my space, my me time and my thoughts, I felt suffocated. However, when he did stay, he would take Star to school and pick her up which made such a huge difference. So even though he was taking a lot from me, the fact that he was giving back some, made it bearable. Nik's name was added to the school register for people with permission to pick Star up from school. He had allocated himself a post and a duty which he knew took a lot of weight off my shoulders. It was working.

During the relationship, I began to notice something that frightened me, a repeat of a historic nightmare. If Nik did not have a drink of alcohol, he suffered from severe withdrawal symptoms. The shakes, sweating, going from hot to cold, bile and mood swings. He did not speak unless spoken to. He lay in the same spot and could not function at all, not even to sit up. It scared me when I first witnessed it. It was not something I had experienced before, but I had read about it.

One night as we were making love, something bizarre happened. As I was about to reach climax, he stopped.

"If I ever catch you doing this with another man, I will kill you. Do you hear me? I will kill you-, he said in a whisper to my ears, then he continued

"Dude, what the hell was that all about?" I quizzed as we lay in each other's arms.

"Yeah, you heard me, I will kill you if you ever let another man get near this" he said as he touched me below. "This, right here, is mine." With that, he went down low and took me in his mouth. I was both excited and confused. I mean who says that, especially in the middle of having sex?

"Why kill me? Why not the guy?

I asked this question carefully, so that I did not trigger anything because to me he had already displayed abnormal behaviour. Something told me he was serious, but I tried to play it down.
"Because it is you who would have given him permission, so for that it's you I kill."

"Well sweetheart, you don't have to worry about that, because this is all yours" I said. It was forgotten for that day, but it became a regular statement during sex. He always had to remind me what would happen to me if he ever caught me with another man. I did not bother about it because I knew it would not happen, I was loyal to him.

I too felt the same although I would not go as far as killing him, but I never wanted him to share what we had, with another woman. Just the thought of it made me crazy. I did not want him to please another woman the same way he did me. I did not want him to have the chemistry that we shared, with another woman. I did not want another woman to enjoy him the way that I did. His body was mine and my body was his. When we made love, we took each other to a land of ecstasy where only he and I existed in everlasting pure love. We lost ourselves in each other. He was not a selfish lover. He was gentle, considerate, and accommodating. So even though he was suffocating me in reality, the nights were full of satisfying pleasure.

My relationship with Nik is what I would call sweet and sour. We were good together but bad for each other. The two of us together were a recipe for disaster; a tragedy waiting to happen. As we got more and more involved, he got more and more possessive and jealous. In his world, his beliefs became his reality. He became very controlling and paranoid about losing me, and that is when it all went wrong.

As time went by, the real Nik began to reveal himself. The nasty and evil person inside him was emerging slowly each day and made my life hell. He bound me with his chains of torture and ridicule. He made me vulnerable and weak so that I could not have the strength to free myself or to think of finding the keys to the chains that bound me so tight. Instead of being his friend and lover, I became his property. He no longer saw me as a human being but as an object, as property, *his* property. He was controlled by this powerful force that in turn wanted to control me. He became a stalker who could not live without his prey.

His drinking was out of control, he was drunk every hour of the day. Alcohol began to play a major part on his mental state. He became more mentally unstable and paranoid. His jealous streak was beginning to come out without restraint. His controlling streak took off to another level. His personal life was not going so smoothly. His ex-wife would deny him access to see his son and he would take it out on me. He would snap for no reason, then apologise. His immigration case was also an issue at the time, and the fact that he was on a very limited income and living in emergency accommodation did not help the situation. So sometimes I made excuses for him tried to understand his situation. I tried to be there for him, but it was affecting me in a very negative way.

One weekend in September 2010 in the evening, as we sat around enjoying family time I came up with an idea.

"Hey, guys, who wants to go to London?!" It was a spur-of-the-moment decision- as soon as I thought it, I decided it. We got ready and packed our bags and were ready to pay my brother a surprise visit. When we arrived at King's Cross train station, I realised that I only had one bar left on my phone battery.

We connected the tube to Hackney and made our way out of the station. I reached out for my phone, but it was completely dead, and my brother's details were in it. We were stuck in the middle of London with no clue where we were going. I had never been to his house before. That evening was going to be the first time. All I knew, was that he lived in Hackney and I knew Hackney well from the time I used to live there. I could not use a pay phone because I had not memorised my brother's mobile number. We were in central Hackney at night in the cold and dark. I knew I had messed up by not checking my phone before we left home_ but then it was a trip made on impulse, which was bad judgement on my part. Nik got really annoyed with me.

"How could you be so stupid? Look at the kids!" he shouted.

"Look I'm sorry I thought I had everything under control. Do you really think I would put my own kids through such situations on purpose? It was_"

"Well, you definitely were not thinking of them, were you?" he cut me off, his face in my face. I was hurt by his words and behaviour, so I pushed him away from me. In a flash, I felt a hot slap on my right cheek. He had struck me! I was in shock. It all happened so fast that it left me mentally paralysed for a few seconds. Apart from the vile text message he had sent me at the time we broke up the first time, he had never spoken any negative word to me, let alone laid his hands on me in anger. My attention went straight to the girls.

"Come here girls it's all right Mummy will sort it," I assured them as I held them both in my arms, still gobsmacked. There was a bed and breakfast a few metres from where we were, so we made our way there hoping there were vacancies. We managed to obtain a family room and went to settle. We were all tired. It was almost midnight and we were lost but we were fortunate enough to find shelter for the night. After eating and putting the girls to sleep, I got ready for bed and climbed in next to Star.

"What are you doing?" he asked. It was the first time either of us had spoken after he slapped me in the face.

"I'm tired, I just want to sleep_," I said to him making myself comfortable.

"Come here, you are not sleeping with Star. You are sleeping in this bed with me", he said quite firmly pointing to the space next to him. I did not want to go against him or to argue, I got up and climbed into bed next to him. He took me into his arms and held me, he began caressing my body and my body was feeling him and the sensation he was giving me. I felt his warm breath against the skin on my neck whilst he gently stroked and explored my body. I burned with desire. I was weak and I was hurting, hurt by him and yet my body was longing for him.

The pain in my heart and the passion in his hands made me very confused. I was furious with him and yet at the same time I wanted him inside me to fulfil my desire for him. When he finally entered me, I almost combusted with pleasure. It was beautiful and passionate, and through his body, I knew he was sorry for his actions. Our bodies and soul communicated with each other. He was truly sorry, and I had forgiven him. No words were spoken, just body and soul. It was the first time of many to follow, that I was caught up in the confusion of the pain of violence and the pleasure of making love.

We had breakfast, packed our bags and headed back home. Without my phone nothing was happening. However, we took advantage of the situation, explored a few central London streets and then had lunch at MacDonald's before boarding the train back home. Things were back to normal. We did not discuss the incident of the previous night. It was as if it had never happened. We carried on as usual and never spoke about it again. It was past and forgotten.

I kept telling myself that if I had not pushed him, he would not have slapped me, so in my head he was justified. He had overreacted, but I had given him a reason. I put my hands on him first because I felt he was in my personal space and using my children to hurt me. Nevertheless, it was water under the bridge. Little did I know, that incident was the beginning of what was going to be a long chain of abusive events.

His attention towards me was no longer sweet but smothering. When he was not with me he would call me over twenty times a day, wanting to know where I was, who I was with or what I was doing. "Why haven't you called me? Did you not miss me?" he would always ask.

"Sweetheart, I was just attending to other stuff around the house you know."

"I miss you so much babe," he would say.

"I miss you too. I will call you back as soon as I settle down. I love you," was my response followed by him declaring his undying love for me and reminding me not to forget to ring him.

"I won't."

But all that conversation might as well never have happened because he would always call me three or four times before I actually settled. It was draining everything inside me. I could never do chores or run errands without being interrupted by a phone call from Nik. If I failed to pick up the calls, the next thing would be a knock on the door. So sometimes I had to entertain his numerous calls just to avoid him coming over.

When he was around, he would get angry when I was on the phone with family or friends, saying that I was neglecting him. I hardly spoke to my family or friends so once in a while when it happened, we would catch up on the times we had missed. But that too was causing problems. He would start to mumble in the background then his voice got louder, forcing me to end my calls. If my phone rang and I did not pick up, he would accuse me of having an affair.

"Who are you trying to avoid? Why aren't you picking up the phone? Because I am here? Who is it!?" he demanded to know.

"Look, I have everyone I need under one roof, so I don't need anyone else. I am not in the mood for talking to people." At times I managed to calm him down but other times he would force me to answer the phone or ring the number back. That was another rule enforced without saying, *'answer your phone at all times'.* He started going through my texts and contacts, asking me about the people he did not recognise or had recently been added. The ones he knew and did not approve of, he deleted.

CHAPTER 5

Towards the end of November 2010 on one afternoon, an associate of ours invited us to their house for their daughter's birthday party. We took the kids, and we all had a wonderful time mingling with different people. On our way back home, Nik went into the off-license and bought himself a three-litre bottle of Ace cider. Then he continued to drink. I prepared the children for bed, read their bedtime stories, tucked them in then I made my way downstairs to join Nik. We watched a bit of television, then I informed him that I was tired and was going to bed. Just as I was about to fall asleep, I heard heavy footsteps coming up the stairs then saw the bedroom door swing open.

"Since when do you come to bed alone without me?"

"What do you mean?" I asked in genuine confusion.

"Whenever you want to sleep, you always say, '*let's go to bed*,' but today you said, '*I am going to bed*'. Is it because you are still hung up on Charlie?
"
"Charlie? Sweetheart what are you talking about?" His eyes opened wide, and veins from his neck started to show.

"Don't think I didn't notice you flirting with Charlie. You were all over him like a lovesick puppy. '*Oh, Charlie, you have beautiful hair, Oh Charlie, this Oh Charlie that,*" he said, mimicking my voice sarcastically. He had introduced me to Charlie as one of his mates from Beaumont Leys. I did compliment him in his lovely looking and well-groomed dreadlocks and had spoken to him a few times during the course of the afternoon. Nik had not mentioned anything about it up until that moment.

"What?" I asked still puzzled.

"I'm talking about you and Charlie. I saw you talking to him and showering him with nonsense compliments!"

"You know what, I am not going to engage myself in an argument with you, not when you are like this. Besides, I am tired and would like to go back to sleep if you don't mind."

"Like what? Huh?" he said as he was walking towards the bed. I saw him take his shoes off, throw them towards the door, then climb into bed fully clothed. I turned the other way and pretended to sleep. Then he began to speak, mouthing off about nothing - while insulting me and accusing me of all sorts. When I did not respond to him, he put his hand on my shoulder and violently shook me to get my attention.

"Hey, I'm talking to you, bitch! Don't ignore me!". He continued belittling me and calling me all sorts of names. He was cursing and pointing right into my face and sometimes making contact.

"You are a whore! You think you're all that, but you are nothing but a sagging hag. You are lucky you have me otherwise who's gonna want a person like you; fat, ugly and old?"

The filthy verbosity went on for hours, and if I did not answer a question, he would shake me and at times order me to face him. He was still drinking his cider. He said some very hurtful words. When I was turned away from him, I wept. He was breaking my heart. This was a side of him that was starting to emerge slowly but surely. My handsome, charming prince had vanished and left me with the monster that lay beside me in my bed. He wore himself out by abusing me and fell asleep. I quickly sneaked out of the bedroom and went to Angel's bed and cried myself to sleep.

I was awoken by a loud thud as my body hit the floor. In confusion and darkness, I saw Nik standing over me and grabbing me from the floor.

"This is not your bedroom!", he said, dragging me out of Angel's room and into my bedroom. He proceeded to shove me onto the bed and lay next to me and fell asleep, holding me in his arms. My confusion deepened and my pain continued. I did not understand how he could claim to love me and yet he was hurting me. How he could switch from being nice, sweet, and gentle to being a total barbarian? I heard him snore, but I dared not move. It was at that point that I realised that I was afraid of him.

Next morning, I was awoken by fingers rubbing me inside my pants and I felt him hard, pressed against my bottom.

"Really?" I snapped. I turned around and looked at him straight in the eyes.

"What?"

"After last night you really expect me to make love to you. I am furious with you. You hurt me really badly_," I said, almost breaking down but I held back the tears because I did not want to give him the satisfaction
.

"What about last night? I didn't touch you."

"You might as well have done; with all the abuse you were throwing at me."

His face showed blank, he did not have a clue what I was talking about. I let it go because I was not about to have a discussion with someone who did not remember anything. I let it go but my heart did not stop hurting, my thoughts did not stop wondering.

"I'm sorry baby," he said to me looking right into my eyes and scooping me into his arms. I felt sorry for him and convinced myself that it was the cider talking. Through his aggression, I saw a vulnerable human being who was insecure but did not want the world to see, so he wore an invisible armour in which he believed. He put all his trust in it and hoped that it would protect him against any situation. I saw a child in him that was dying to be loved and cared for. A child who had lost trust and faith in humanity. I wanted him to know that I was there if he needed me. I wanted to help him, to love and care for him. To make the pain go away, I let him make love to me and soon the pain was replaced with pleasure.

But this was not going to be the last time I took a beating over Charlie. One summer afternoon of June 2011, we got ourselves ready for a day at the park. It was a well-known park near the city centre where people could bar-b-que and play music. We prepared our food, meat, our instant bar-be-que, coal, and gadgets, and we set off.

It was a beautiful day, and the park was busy with people sitting in groups having fun and drinking and children playing on the rides. All was going well. Nik and I had spread out a blanket where we lay the food and sat. We were playing music from my Bluetooth speaker and he was taking care of the meat. We laughed and joked and occasionally I would go and play with the kids. At that time, Nik was recovering from a leg injury he had sustained a couple of weeks earlier in Birmingham.

The story goes that he and his mate whom he met at the hostel decided to sneak out to go and purchase some alcohol. As he jumped over the fence on his way back, he lost his balance and fell to the ground, causing a fracture to his foot. His leg had been in plaster since then and he had a couple more weeks to go, so he was not as mobile as he would have loved to be. People we recognised would pass by, engage in chit-chat and move on.

Towards the end of the day, the groups were beginning to disperse, and the music was dying down. We decided then it was time to go home so we started packing our stuff. We noticed at the other end of the park that there were preparations for a football match. We began to walk towards Nikolas's flat which was about a ten-minute walk away; he was using his crutches. We were walking to the exit gates towards the football crowd. Amongst the crowd, I noticed Charlie. Our eyes met, and we smiled then proceeded to meet and we embraced.

As we were walking, Nik was a few feet ahead of me with Star, and I was walking behind with Angel. The moment our arms opened for a hug, Nik turned at that very moment and saw me giving Charlie a hug. All hell broke loose. The expression on his face changed, he turned around and began charging towards me. I let go of Charlie and turned to run the way we had come. I looked back and saw him running after me. To my amazement, he did the unthinkable-: he ditched the crutches because they were slowing him down.

He continued chasing me around the field whilst everybody just stood there doing nothing. He got to one of his crutches, picked it up and threw it at me but it missed. He lost his balance and fell and that is when I stopped running. I was out of breath, I looked around and saw people in chaos, then I thought to myself, "*they all watched him come after me and none of them did anything, not even Charlie"*. And yet, there he was, helping Nik back on his feet and onto his crutches. I grabbed the girls immediately and phoned for a taxi which was already waiting for us at the entrance. When we finally got there. I took my children home.

A couple of hours later I was sitting with the girls in the lounge watching cartoons, when I heard a noise coming from the kitchen. I stood up and went to investigate. My heart missed a beat when I bumped into Nik. My kitchen door was wide open.

"What are you doing here? How did you get in?"

I was petrified. I did not know what he was going to do. His behaviour had become erratic and unpredictable lately, so I did not know what to expect. We got into an altercation, I wanted him to leave and he was refusing to do so. Throwing Charlie's name in my face, calling me a whore, prostitute, and anything ugly he could think of. I opened the front door and gestured for him to leave but he refused. As I turned away from him to make my way upstairs, he struck me on the side of my head with his crutch.

"Don't you walk away from me!" I saw stars and the world went blank for a while. I opened my eyes and saw him standing over me and in the doorway of the lounge, stood my three-year-old who had witnessed it all. I got myself up and took Star's hand to lead her to her bedroom upstairs,

Angel was already in her room. She did not like it when Nik and I engaged in loud arguments. She retreated into her bedroom which was her sanctuary. I made sure both girls were settled in bed and went to the mirror in the bathroom. I had a big lump on my temple, and my head hurt like hell. I took a deep breath and made my way downstairs.

"The police are on their way, so if I were you, I would make myself scarce before they get here". I said in a low and calm voice, standing about a metre away from him.

"Bitch! You called the police on me! Fuck you!" he raved as he shoved me against the wall, walking past me in the hallway and to the front door. I heard the door slam, and I howled.

"Why, oh Lord, why? Why? Why? Why? Why? Why?" I wept.

While he was injured, his crutches became a common weapon against me. Two weeks after the Charlie incident - after several calls and several threats on his part to come over. I finally gave in and went to visit him at the hostel in Birmingham. I asked Nina to look after the girls because I was not sure how things would turn out with Nik. All was well; I met him at the hostel, and we went to buy a bottle of whisky and coke and sat in the park drinking and talking. It was fine at first until Charlie's name popped up again and others that I did not know of. We argued so I stood up to walk away and he followed me. He followed me all the way to the bus stop and hopped on the same bus where we kept arguing, causing a right scene.

I got off the bus and so did he. He was still in pursuit. By this time, I was no longer responding to him, but that did not keep him quiet. Sometimes he would use the end of his crutch to poke me to get my attention. I managed to evade him when he stopped briefly to speak to some guy. Amongst the crowd I could see him, in a frenzy looking for me, I kept my eyes on him but remained out of his sight. I had full view of the train station and the bus station; but was afraid to move into vision in case he spotted me. After a while I could no longer see him so he could have been anywhere. I had been there for over an hour, so I convinced myself that by then, he must have got tired and returned to the hostel. I emerged slowly from my hiding place and began to walk carefully across the street to the train station, all the while looking around to see if he was still about.

The coast seemed to be clear, so I took a deep sigh and relaxed my shoulders, which were tense with fear. I reached out into my handbag and took out a box of cigarettes, I looked for my lighter but could not find it. It was then that noticed the gentleman standing next to me was smoking so I politely asked for a lighter and he was kind enough to offer it. He too was also waiting for a train to Leicester, so we engaged in a casual chit-chat, and soon my troubles were forgotten, I was going home to my children whom I had been talking about to him when I felt a hard impact on my back followed by an excruciating pain that travelled down my spine.

"This is why you were in a hurry to get away from me!" Everything happened so fast; the gentleman I was speaking to, took off immediately after I was struck with a crutch on my back. I also, without much thought, ran towards the station entrance and down the stairs to my platform. I was overcome with astonishment. I could not comprehend what was going on. I was in a stupor and could not hold back the tears. I did not understand why Nik was behaving that way towards me and yet each day he declared his love for me. He was so brazen as to attack me in a public place in broad day light.

I drank whisky the whole journey from Birmingham to Leicester. It was a weekend so I knew Nina would stay over and help look after the children. I was in despair. I needed help. I needed to get away, but I seemed to be tangled in a web of poisonous love. It tasted deceitfully sweet, but it was extremely lethal. My heart was aching and so were my bones and flesh from the times I had been struck hard with a crutch. When I went to use the train toilets, I looked in the mirror and saw the visible bump on my temple which I had managed to hide so well from people by combing my hair to the front. Another reminder of the cruel reality I was living under.

Nina was my best friend to whom I told everything, but I did not tell her about this incident and others that came after that. If she were not there to witness it, I did not tell her. I was embarrassed and too ashamed. How had I allowed myself to be so weak and so manipulated? I had never ever been frightened of a human being the way I feared Nik. He had managed to mould me into his property that he could use and abuse. He made and changed rules as we went along. So just before I left the train, I fixed my hair and face. When I got home, I pretended that I had had an amazing time and that all was well. But deep down, I was dying.

~ ~ ~

We let life continue, but both my body and mind were tiring. Nik was taking up much of my time and space. He stayed for long periods and it was fatiguing, especially with his drinking. I noticed that I was also starting to drink more than I should have been. My world was a mess and I was trying to find ways to sort it out. Other times I just wanted to forget the mess for a while, so I drowned my sorrows in alcohol, although I never drank during week days because I needed to manage the children's weekly routine.

Each time I tried to bring the topic up he would joke about me wanting to get rid of him so I could bring another man home. He made it seem like a joke, but I knew he was not kidding. The reason why he did not want to leave was that he wanted to keep an eye on me. He liked to monitor the people I saw, spoke to and where I went. Being away from me and not knowing what I was up to made him go crazy. He would let his imagination take him to the dark side, and he was making sure he took me with him.

"You know I could never do that to my girls. What example would I be setting if I were to bring different men here? I respect my children, and as far as they know, you are the only man that sleeps in their mummy's bed." I would always assure him.

I was losing control of the situation. Nik was taking over my life and my position in the house. I could see it happening and yet I found no courage to confront it. Whenever I told myself that I was going to talk to him, I would go over and over it in my head, trying to imagine how the words should come out. The more I rehearsed, the more I got agitated and unable to speak. The more I did not speak, the more he began to stay; the closer I was getting to falling down.

One afternoon, Nina came to visit, and we were chilling in the lounge. Nik and I got into a disagreement and he went upstairs. I stayed with Nina for a while then I asked her to look after the children whilst I went to our friend's house just five doors down. I was drinking and I wanted to drink some more, Nina did not drink so I went to my drinking buddies next door. I wanted to get away from the house which had now become a sad place to be. My house was no longer homely, it had become a house of torture.

Seth and Mika were well known in the neighbourhood as the alcoholics of the boulevard. Once in a while, I would go over to their house whenever I wanted some drinking company and, sometimes, they would come to me. They were drunks but were such a lovely couple with warm hearts. Seth was twenty years her junior, but they somehow made it work. I took my wine and knocked on their door. They welcomed me with open arms. I made myself comfortable and we drank, talked, and laughed. They kept telling me to stay away from Nik and that he was bad news. I tried to explain my situation to them, and they even offered to come over to remove Nik from my property. I did not want any drama, so I let it go. I realised that I was drunk, so I asked them to walk me home even though it was only a few yards away. It had just gone after seven pm.

Just as we were walking out of their gate, we saw Nik coming out of my gate charging towards us. I had Seth and Mika on either side of me, and when Nik reached us, he grabbed my arm and pulled me away causing me to lose my balance and fall face down on the pavement, grazing my face. I blacked out for a couple of minutes, and when I came to, there was a lot of commotion around me. Mika was on the phone with the police and Nina was shouting out my name, Seth and Nik were wrestling with each other. I shook my head and got up and when I heard Mika on the phone, I grabbed the phone from her and cut the call.

"No police!" I screamed.

"We have rung the ambulance as well they are on their way," related Mika who was now holding on to Nik making sure he did not get away before the police arrived. Mika was a strong woman, six-foot tall and had served in the

British army for ten years before she was let go and became an alcoholic.

"Look guys I don't need the police and I don't need no ambulance. I am home now so you guys can go now. I will be fine."

"Darling you are badly hurt you really must go to the hospital." During the chaos, Leo's BMW pulled up. He got out of the car and took one look at me. "Oh my Goodness!" he exclaimed with eyes wide open and wearing a horrified face.

"Nik, did this?" he asked, turning to Mika, who confirmed it. I got myself away from the fracas and went inside where I met with my children, oblivious to the state of my face. I could feel some tingling and some blood trickling but otherwise I felt good. Moments later I saw five police officers enter my lounge where I was seated. When the first one looked at me, he immediately turned away to his colleagues and I heard them speak in low voices. Then he turned back to me whilst the other officers spoke to the rest of them.

"Miss Wallace, can you tell me what happened? How did you sustain those injuries?" he asked with his note book out. I refused to co-operate and when they asked me if I wanted to press charges, I refused that too. When I saw them cuff Nik, I stood up from the sofa and tried to prevent them from doing it, but I was overpowered. Everyone around me told me how badly hurt I was and that I needed medical attention. I stood up and walked towards the mirror. It was as if a heavy object hit me in my guts and I reeled backwards.

I could hear my heartbeat and felt the fast rhythm in my chest. I moved forward against the mirror to find a horrifying picture staring back at me. I looked like something Frankenstein might have created. My face was swollen up like a balloon. The whole right side had been scraped and bruised and my right eye was completely shut. My lips had small cuts and were bleeding slightly. I also sustained superficial cuts and scrapes on my right hand and knees. It was a picture from a horror movie.

"Oh my goodness! Did I let my daughter see me like this?" She must have been terrified, I was petrified.

Upon seeing that image, I agreed to go to hospital, and the ambulance came for me. Mika and Seth went back home, Nina stayed to look after the girls and after a few angry words, Leo took off.

"The guy is my friend, and you know I love him to bits, but he is in an asshole. Why do you put up with his behaviour? The guy is a loser, look how much trouble he has caused you so far. Your car was towed twice, because of him, now this? What's next? Your children? Is that when you will leave him? When they come for your children?" He squeezed his lips together and walked away, leaving me with deep words and food for thought.

Next morning when Angel came into my bedroom, I could tell things were not looking good. She came into my bed and kept looking at me without taking her eyes off my face. She was humming in a low voice as she sat beside me. Normally, she would walk in, check on me, then walk out again and Angel was not one to be touched by many things. So her behaviour made me wake up to reality. Star had seen my injuries the previous day, so she was not too shocked by it all when she walked in. I could tell she was terror-stricken, but she was trying to be brave for me.

"Don't worry, Mum, you still look beautiful" she said as she lay next to me.

That was the most beautiful thing I had ever heard. It literally made the hurt go away. I rang Joan to ask her to pick up Star that morning for the school run. I was not about to expose myself as a battered woman to other parents. Once the children were gone, I headed to town to buy myself a pair of large dark glasses and a wig that covered half my face. On the way, people kept asking me if I was involved in a car accident; apparently, that is how serious the injuries were. The night before I even overheard one of the police officers say, "We are dealing with a very dangerous situation here'.

When I came back home, I saw Nik sitting outside by the door. I did not react because I did not know how I felt. All I knew was that I was very saddened and scarred by his actions. He came in and spoke, refusing to take responsibility for his actions.

"I didn't do anything to you; why don't you ask your friends Mika and Seth they were the ones with you when you got hurt. I was trying to protect you from those junkies, they are not good for you. I keep telling you to stay away from them". He justified his behaviour by putting the blame on everybody else but himself.

I could not believe it; he was not sorry at all.

"All I did was pull you and you lost your balance and fell because you were too drunk." He went on trying to justify the results and minimise his role. I had taken pictures of my face the night before and he reached for my phone and deleted them all. My injuries took over two months to completely heal and fade.

It was after that incident that social services became involved in our lives. The beginning of another battle that I was to fight on my own, this time, against more powerful and more resourceful adversaries. I stood no chance. The very people I had been fighting to protect all their lives were the ones who were at risk of being taken away from me. My children were my world. I would die without them. The devastation I felt was unimaginable. There was a lot to take in, I felt as though my head were about to explode.

Deep down I felt empathy for him; he was a tormented soul. I imagined it was not fun to have such a destructive addiction. I often heard people say that addiction is a choice. I had never looked at it from that perspective. Addiction is a tormenter. People affected by it need help and I was there trying to help Nik. Deep down there was a loving and caring gentleman, but alcohol always brought out the beast in him. It made him selfish and vile. He became the devil himself. I felt as if I was in a relationship with two people.

He would time how long it took me to go the shops and back. If I came back a few minutes late according to his calculations, I would have to account for the minutes. He would ring my phone to find out where I was and why I was taking so long. My watch would tell me that I had only been away for fifteen minutes and yet it was already causing a frenzy, which led to verbal attacks, abuse and, at times, a shove against the wall or floor.

I convinced myself that he was just under a lot of stress and was finding his situation with his son and immigration problems too difficult, so that was why he was lashing out. I told myself he did not mean to hurt me; that he could never hurt me deliberately. He loved me, so we soldiered on with our partnership. He showed me he was sorry by his ability to communicate with me without speaking. Any wrongdoings were erased in those moments. Pain and anger were replaced by the feeling of love and pleasure. Apologies were expressed not by words, but through lovemaking, a language only the body and soul could understand.

From the day of my face injuries, Leo always dropped by to check on us. One day he came by when Nik was away. I invited him in, and we sat and talked. We engaged in all sorts of topics from, politics to relationships, religion, you name it. He was quite an intelligent guy, and I enjoyed engaging him in conversation. He was worldly, and that also helped with widening my horizon. Later we took the girls to the shops to get them some treats and then we decided to get a few beers for ourselves and went back to my house where we continued to chat and laugh. Not only was he knowledgeable, he also had a great sense of humour. I had a wonderful afternoon.

When Nik came by, I just so happened to mention my afternoon with Leo and trying to tell him I had a lovely time, but he before I could finish, he cut me off.

"What was he doing here?" he demanded to know.

"I didn't think you would mind. He said he was ..." I was cut off before I could finish my sentence.

"Exactly, you didn't think! Do you think right now if I went to his house and he wasn't in, his wife would invite me in?" He was shouting at the top of his voice.

"Why are you getting angry? He is your friend and I was being polite."

"Polite? Is that what you are calling spending the afternoon with my best friend drinking beer? Just the two of you chilling?" His eyes had widened, the veins on his neck became visible as we stood near the inside of the bedroom door. Then he started calling me all sorts of names, coming right up my face with fire blazing in his eyes.

"I think you should leave now please_," I said to him.

"Bitch, are you crazy? Where do you expect me to go at this time of night?"

"Well then stop disrespecting me in my own home!" I said angrily.

"You are a fucking whore!" he said to me as he walked past me, shoving me against the bedroom wall. I heard the loud thud from the impact of my head hitting the wall, then I hit my elbow against the desk as I tumbled down. I heard him walk downstairs and then heard sounds from the kitchen. My head was pounding and so were my elbow and back. He did not even stop to see if I was hurt. He watched me smash into the wall and onto the floor and he walked away without a care in the world. I was in pain, but I managed to drag myself onto the bed and sat on the edge trying to comprehend what had just happened. The abuse was continuing yet I was doing nothing about it. I did not know what to do. I just wanted it to stop.

The next time Leo came over, he brought his wife Marcy with him. It was a wonderful evening, and everyone was in a cheerful mood. We were all engaging well with each other. After dinner, the four of us sat in my living room, enjoying a quiet evening and a drink. Nik began to make awkward remarks. The words were inaudible; as if he were talking to himself but at the same time sending a message across. He was drinking heavily.

"Don't think I can't see what's going on. I see it all. You think I am stupid, but I will show you that I am well ahead of you."

These were just statements being thrown out there, not directed to anyone in particular but were loud enough to be heard. I knew what was going, on but was not entertaining him. It went on for a while, then suddenly from out of the blue, he stood up from his seat, which was next to mine and opposite Leo and his wife. He charged across the table towards Leo bursting into a manic frenzy.

"Stop looking at my wife! I have been watching you staring at my wife all evening. Why don't you look at your own wife who is sitting right beside you? Why do you keep looking at Nicolette!?"

And with that the party was over. Even Marcy thought it was ridiculous, so they left. Then his attention turned to me. Fortunately, the children were upstairs asleep. He was screaming and shouting at me, following behind me as I cleared the living room and tidied the kitchen. I did not respond, even when he grabbed me by the arm or poked me to get my attention. I was getting so angry I was almost exploding, but I knew that if I lashed out it would only make the situation worse.

"Oh, you are ignoring me, let's see if you will ignore this..." he said as he entered the living room.

Moments later the speakers blasted with loud music_, he had turned on the music to maximum volume, knowing, it would wake the kids and annoy the neighbours. I went to the lounge and switched the hi-fi off. He turned it on again on full blast. We did this to and fro several times until he shoved me against the wall where I bashed my head. However, that was the least of my worries. My children were upstairs, and I had the neighbours to consider. I had a powerful system; I could see the pictures on the wall vibrating from the sound. Each time I tried to get to the sound system, he blocked me and pushed me, causing me to fall back onto the floor.

"Enough is enough!" I screamed. I got up and marched to the kitchen where I dialled 999 from my mobile. Somehow, he heard me on the phone to the police, and he lowered the volume and started shouting over me to the operator. He fled the scene before the police got there and took the house keys with him.

That was my first call to the police to report the violence that was going on behind the scenes. Even though I told the officer that I had been assaulted and even though the dispatchers themselves recorded that they heard the ex in the background saying, " *she hit him first*", they recorded the incident as a_ **'no offences have taken place'**. They did not see any injuries, and the aggressor had left the scene. Not only that, I reported that he had taken away my house keys, but they made no effort to make us safe. I had just reported to the police that I had been assaulted in my own home with my vulnerable children in the house and the perpetrator had fled with my house keys, but they did nothing. I would have expected them to either put us in a safe place for the night until my keys were recovered or arrange to change the locks. They instructed me to call them again in case he returned; well, of course he was going to return, he had the house keys! I felt let down, and it was one of many such incidents that followed.

CHAPTER 6

The brutality continued, so did the unpredictable outbursts and the fits of rage. The jealousy and paranoia worsened and so did his drinking. He then began with the criticism; I could no longer do anything right. My new hairstyle did not suit me, so he picked up a hairdo for me. *'That dress makes you look old.' 'Are you going out looking like that?' Your hair doesn't suit you, look at yourself in the mirror, you are a mess! Oh, I didn't know people still wore those! Ha!-ha!-ha!'* Those were some of the remarks I had to put up with.

Soon, he started stalking me. He just always used to appear wherever I happened to be. He knew who came in and out of my house and on what dates and which times. He described the clothes I wore on certain days; it was creepy. However, in a crazy sort of way, I thought it was cute that he was so hung on me. That he would invest all his time just to watch me and learn more about me, no one had ever done that for me before. I grew up alone and never had any meaningful relationship and so for years I had been deprived of affection and attention. In a sick sort of twisted way, I found it fascinating and daunting at the same time.

No man was allowed to look at me on the street and if they did, it was my fault. I had done something to attract the man's attention. If I greeted someone on the streets, that warranted trouble; he would grill me on how I knew the person and whether I was cheating on him. His belief that

I was cheating on him grew extensively. He often accused me of having affairs with his friends. This was a very dark period indeed. And although he would push and hold me down or against the wall, I never telephoned the police. I was afraid of losing my children.

Having social services in my life meant that I was no longer allowed to have any contact with Nikolas Martins and if he turned up at the property, I had to call the police immediately. Each call to the police meant a record with social services, and I wanted to avoid that. I would have unannounced visits from social services twice or three times a month, just to check on the situation. Whenever the social worker came, everything was running smoothly. He never found Nik in the house and he never found me drinking. As far as that relationship was going, I wanted to keep it that way. I was not going to add any more information to their record on file.

On one occasion, Nikolas turned up whilst I was on a call to the operator at ten minutes to eight at night and yet it took the police one-and-a-half hours to reach me - even though I had expressed my fear to the operator. I was too scared and that was the reason why I was whispering. The call ended abruptly because I was going to hide away. In their own record they state that they were trying to ring my mobile several times and yet it took them so long to arrive at the scene.

They were aware that I had two vulnerable children in the house, and I reported that someone had deliberately broken my window. The damage to the window was from the inside, and when I told the police that I suspected that Nik had been in the house, they told me there was no proof of entry. My dining room window was broken, it had been smashed from the inside and there was glass all over the dining floor. The incident took over five hours to be resolved, and it was exhausting both physically and mentally.

There was never a follow-up regarding this matter; no arrests were made, and the case was closed. However, I managed to have the window fixed by the council without incurring any charges because it was damage caused during the commission of a crime. Life went on painfully. Being with me made him feel important and a victor. He felt needed and found an opportunity to pounce and take control. He used control to validate his own importance.

I had fallen deeply in love with him, but his intensity frightened me. It was as thrilling as it was terrifying. The reality of who I was , had been thrown out of the window, causing me to lose touch with reality. My mind often wandered in a maze of distorted thoughts. I thought about my two beautiful girls and I was torn apart. Oscar Wilde once said, *"To lose one parent maybe regarded as misfortune, but to lose both parents looks like carelessness".* I was losing touch with reality and yet my children were part of that reality.

I remember his late-night visits, where he would turn up unannounced and highly intoxicated, banging and kicking the door, shouting obscene profanities and waking up the whole neighbourhood. He never considered the girls sleeping upstairs. There were many incidents like this. Most went unreported, unless one of the neighbours rang the police. The time-frame from the initial call to despatch, was too exhausting and stressful. My energy was already being sucked out by the volatile situation I found myself entangled in.

He kept knocking at odd hours, banging the door, and flapping the letter box and neighbours would alert the police. Sometimes I would find him slumped in the back garden. At other times he would gain entry by climbing through the bathroom window using the drainpipe and the shed as support. Other times, because of the exhaustion and the consequences of dealing with the neighbours and the police, I would let him in. He knew that window would almost likely be open because that is where I smoked at night. I would be awoken by cosmetics falling into the tub and floor and it would scare the hell out of me.

Loneliness left me vulnerable, grasping at the first sign of love and understanding; shown to me, I would feel on top of the world. But then that feeling was ripped away, leaving me lonely yet again and frustrated. I could sense myself drifting towards darkness and desperation. I loved Nik with all my heart, but he was not the person I expected him to be. A lot of people had warned me against him. His own best friend Marnie, and his wife Lisa, would often talk about how Nik mistreated his ex-wife and that he would laugh about it. My friends warned me, his friends warned me, but it fell on deaf ears.

~ ~ ~

Around March of 2012 Marnie, Nina, Nik, and I were chilling one evening drinking and chatting as usual_, except for Nina who did not drink. The evening was going smoothly; when Marnie was around, Nik, hardly caused any drama. I guess it was a side of him he did not want to show his best friend, who had known him for years. So with Marnie around, I did not fear much, I was more relaxed with Nik and I both drinking. Marnie could not handle his drink, though and each time he drank, he ended up sleeping which he did on this particular night. He fell asleep on the couch and we were mocking him.

I went into the kitchen to prepare some snacks, and brought back a rack of ribs, some samosas, and a few other nibbles. After chatting for a bit I went to the kitchen to get a drink and Nina followed me. She had a prank for Marnie. She decided we should strip him naked whilst he was passed out so as to see his reaction when he came round. I thought it was funny and I was up for it. We got back in the lounge where Nik was enjoying his ribs unaware of our little trick.

I walked towards the sofa they were both on, and we both grabbed his hands while trying to take his shirt off. We were giggling. Before I knew it, I saw a rib bone flying across the room hitting me just below my left eye.

"What the fuck do you think you are doing!" Nik shouted as he threw his plate on the table and walked towards me.

"What the hell!" I said in shock, running my fingers down my face to feel the damage.

"Hey Nik!" Nina screamed. "What's wrong with you? We are only playing."

She too was taken aback by his behaviour. He had so much rage in him that because he could not reach me, he had to use the nearest weapon; rib bone in hand. He was that desperate to hurt me. Marnie woke up amid the commotion and we told him what had happened. I felt so humiliated in front of friends. Worse still, I was being violated in my own home and I had no one to protect me. I had a deep cut on my face; another reminder of the savagery I was going through.

I did not call the police, and I did not ask him to leave. I had no faith in the system, and I had no strength to fight him. Instead, I let him do what he always did to make it feel better, make sweet love to me. It was the only comfort I had besides my children. My time with the children was being affected; I was too sad to play with them sometimes. So I would buy them new games or DVDs to keep them engaged and entertained when I could not do it. When they went to bed I stayed up, drinking, and crying.

I always prayed to God to continue giving me the strength and motivation to keep caring for my children and thanks to Him I was managing. Emotionally and mentally I was struggling but I physically pushed myself to make sure my children were bathed, fed and taken to school presentably. They both progressed in school. I always made time for their development and education. However, I wished I could do more, but I was slowly dying inside. I had to endure his unpredictable behaviour and violent outbursts.

Nik and I had put the girls to bed one night, then decided to chill upstairs in the bedroom. We put on our favourite movie, *'The Last King Of Scotland,'* and we were drinking and chatting away. We laughed and mimicked the character of Idi Amin which we enjoyed doing even when we were not watching the movie.

"Besides me, if you were to pick someone to have sex with, who would it be?" I asked in a playful mood.

"Joan", he answered without even giving it a thought. My chest felt heavy as if I had been hit by a solid object.

"Joan? my friend Jo?" I asked, still flabbergasted by his swift answer.

All he did was give this smirky smile and that hurt even more. *He wants to fuck Jo!? Of all people!* I took offence and I was hurt because Jo was one of my close friends and they saw each other almost daily during school runs. My mind was on fast forward and so was my heart, so I decided to hit back.

"For me, it would be Teddy."

Before I knew it I was rolling from the bed and on to the floor after crashing against the wardrobe. I had a punch thrown in my face that sent me flying. When I landed on the floor I pretended to pass out. The blow was unexpected; the reaction was not anticipated, and my mind was still racing with the thought of him and Joan in bed together. It was all too much I needed to step back.

"Sweetheart, hey, sweetheart can you hear me wake up".

He had got out of bed and was trying to revive me, but I kept still.

"Oh baby, please wake up. I'm sorry".

He started kissing me all over my face and body and then he lifted me onto the bed where he continued to apologise and kiss me. After a while I pretended to come round.

"Hey, sweetie, I am so sorry. Please forgive me," he said as he fondled me. After that we continued drinking, I was drinking because I could not cope with the situation any more. And then it all started again.

He started interrogating me about his brother, when I started having feelings for him and how tacky I was. The more he drank the more unreasonable and aggressive he became. The more his behaviour escalated, the more I drank. Alcohol was going to be my shield. When I drank, I could stand up to him. I could talk back. Not only that, I just did not want to feel half the emotions I was feeling, so I had to numb some nerves. He was hurting me with his words, so I decided to take it further.

"You might never know, I may have already fucked him!" I said, followed by a sarcastic laugh.

What started off as a peaceful night became mayhem. He began throwing punches at me and swearing, calling me all sorts of horrible names one can think of. All I did was try to block his punches by cowering or kicking with my legs. He was getting louder and so were my screams to make him stop. The children were asleep, but I knew by then they would probably be awoken by the commotion. The punches continued and so did the castigations. He would take a break in between to gulp his drink. I got my chance when he left to go to the bathroom, I ran into my younger daughter's bedroom. I saw her sitting up on her bed and lifted her up to cuddle her and tell her all would be well. Suddenly I saw the bedroom door swing open.

"Bitch!" he said as he took a swing at me.

I managed to dodge him, and he narrowly missed my daughter who I was still holding in my arms. That shocked me to the core. His fist brushed my daughter's arm, hitting me on top of my head. I immediately put my baby down and pushed him out, then, closed the door behind me. By now he had calmed down considerably, I am not sure if he had realised what had just happened.

"I want you to leave now!" I shouted.

He did not say a thing. He just got his things together and walked out. I went to Star and held her and while apologising gravely for what she had witnessed. I felt so rotten inside for putting my baby in harm's way. If I had not ducked in time, that blow could have landed on my beloved little girl. I can honestly say from the bottom of my heart, I never expected that from Nik, even though I knew he could be extreme. This incident showed me that he was willing to go to any level, to maintain his control and rule over me. I put her back to sleep and went down to the kitchen where I opened a bottle of wine to drown my sorrows. It was already the early hours of the morning.

There was a charity event going on at Angel's school the next afternoon and I had promised to take both girls I had already bought tickets a week prior, but now I did not have the energy or motivation. I had spent hours being kicked, punched and verbally ridiculed. He had almost hurt my daughter and that was the feeling I was failing to get rid of. The GUILT. It was tearing me apart. All I could think was, *what if?* But in my head, it was no longer a *'what if'* because he *did* make contact with my daughter_ even though it was just a brush. I was responsible, I had failed to be her protector; the main responsibility of a mother. I held myself accountable and yet I kept self-medicating with poison

.

I got lost in the alcohol and in the dark maze of my thoughts. Before I knew it, it was light outside. I looked at the clock and it had just gone after six am. I poured the last wine that remained in my glass down the sink and started cleaning. I had to be ready and fit for the afternoon event. I had promised and prepared the girls for the event. I could not let them down, I was not going to let Nik spoil another day for them. I checked on the girls who were fast asleep then I went to take the trash out. Just as I was walking back in I saw a foot near the door. Nik was back! I could not believe it. His presence alone troubled me. His darkness over-shadowed me. I resented him. He wanted to apologise and talk and fix things, which I thought was hilarious.

I asked him to leave, but he would not. I was too exhausted to fight so I rang his mother and told her what was going on. I thought maybe she could talk some sense into him and get him to leave us alone but that did not work. So I rang his ex-wife and told her what had occurred the night before. I handed the phone to him. I heard her threaten him that if he would not leave, he will not see his son ever again and that she would ring social services. Thank God, that made him think, and he left, but he still left me rattled. He could turn up at any time. I did not even know whether he had truly gone or if he had been watching the house the whole time.

Because the girls were looking forward to the fete, I had to take them, but it was difficult. I drank most of the night before, and I was physically and emotionally aching. My mind was spinning like a whirlwind, but I had to get myself together. We got ready and did not stop until we all looked presentable, as if all were going well. I was finding it really hard to mingle. I had a lot on my mind. I needed a break away from everything just to be able to revive myself. But life had to carry on, fit or unfit. The children needed me. We arrived at the school just after twelve pm and I asked the taxi driver to pick us up at five pm.

Around three-thirty pm I was called into the headteacher's office.

"It has been brought to my attention by another member of staff that your breath smells of alcohol," she said.
"I am not drinking if that's what you are asking me." I responded.

"That's not the point. The point is that you have been drinking whilst in charge of the children, and even I can smell it on your breath", she replied.

Please, God, this is not happening. What is happening?

"I am sorry, but I cannot let you look after the children without someone else with you," she continued. My world was spinning. I felt arrows being thrown at me left right and centre. I felt under attack, as if the whole world were closing in on me. I couldn't breathe. I felt as if I were going to faint. The emotions I felt at that moment were overwhelming. The fear was crushing every bone in my body.

"You are taking my children?!" I asked as I stood up as the tears rolled down my cheeks.

"You can't do that! Have I displayed any behaviour that led you to think that my children might be at risk? I have been here over three hours with my children, and you said nothing!"

I was upset and my emotions were running high, but she remained calmly seated in her chair. She was adamant that she was not going to release the children to me unless I had someone else look after them. I was gutted, my world was crumbling right before me. My children were my world, I could not let anyone take them away from me. I told myself to calm down and not make the situation worse; I had to think fast. I was pacing up and down trying to control my breathing. It was a struggle. I took my mobile phone out of my bag and dialled Nina's number, but there was no answer. I tried Joan but it went straight to voicemail. I kept trying them, and the more I failed to get a response, the more agitated and desperate I became.

I sat down with the headteacher and opened up about what had been going on. She already knew that social services were involved and knew about the domestic violence that was going on. So I told her exactly what had happed the previous night and left out, of course, the part that Nik had missed hitting my daughter by an inch. She said she understood, but still would not give me my children. I was getting angry and frustrated. I went outside and continued to ring Joan and Nina's numbers, but - was still not able to reach them. I just kept walking and crying. My mind was out of control. I began to have visions of terror as if I were hallucinating. I was picturing them taking my children away and them screaming for me with their hands stretched out trying to reach me as they are led away. It was awful.

Soon I arrived at Joan's house, which was ten minutes away. I buzzed and buzzed, but there was no-one home. I felt my heart deflating. Eventually, I turned around and started making my way to Nina's, which was another twenty minutes walk. There too, there was no answer. I could not get hold of either of my friends, the only two people I could have relied on to take care of my children. I was wandering the streets in tears. I did not even hide my distress_, I could not even if I had tried. I was losing my life; I was entering a tragedy, and I was scared. By the time I got back to school, it was deserted. The fete was over, and everyone had cleared off, including my children. That was it for me at that moment.

My whole world was covered with a very grey cloud; it was about to shower on me heavily, I could see the storm brewing. I was all alone at a deserted school with no idea where they had taken my children. I had nowhere to go and no one to turn to. The pain in my heart felt as if someone was repeatedly twisting a knife through it. I threw myself to the ground and sat there weeping for a while until I came up with a plan. But my mind had taken in too much. At that moment I felt very vulnerable. I wanted someone to hold me and tell me that everything would be okay and that there had been a misunderstanding, and all would be well. Or simply just to wake up from what seemed to be a nightmare.

"Hello, taxi please from East Gate School to Upperton Road. For now please". The taxi came within minutes, and I was soon at a house in Upperton Road. I was buzzed in and walked upstairs.

"They took my children…" I said as I collapsed into Nik's arms.

"What? What you talking about?"

"They took my babies!" I cried. He tied to calm me down and get to make me explain what had happened.

"I have a taxi waiting outside I just didn't know what else to do or where to go", I said to him still in distress. He put his shoes on and came with me into the taxi then we went home together. By then I was a bit calmer. He was trying as hard as he could to calm me down. I explained to him what had happened and then he suggested we call the police, which I did. I reported the matter to the police and asked them to investigate the whereabouts of my children. They told me to stay at home and wait for a phone call. I was broken; empty and almost delirious.

There were telephone calls back and forth between social services and police, and it was doing my head in. I went into the kitchen and brought back a bottle of wine and a glass, but Nik immediately grabbed it away from me.

"This is the last thing you want right now. You need to stay sober. You don't want the authorities to come here and see you drunk, do you? In fact, I am going to the shops to buy you soda water to clear your system," which he did. He was stepping up and saying the right words. It was like having my old Nik back. He showed empathy and concern, and it all looked genuine and sincere to me at the time. During the evening, I had managed to clarify that I had not misplaced my children, but that they were being withheld from me and that I was trying to find someone to help with care. The police received a report that a mother had lost her children.

The police came around the house for a formal statement and obviously to assess the situation. Nik had to hide in the shed because he was not meant to be at the address. A few hours later, two social workers turned up and asked to inspect the house. They went upstairs to the children's bedrooms and then came downstairs to address me.

"You have a very lovely home, and I am quite impressed with the children's bedrooms. Sorry about the misunderstanding, we received a report saying that you had abandoned your children at East Gate school and that is how we got involved. The children have been taken to a foster home, but we are satisfied that they can return home as I see no risks."

I did not understand how wrong information could be passed on and how the misunderstanding came about, but these were authorities working under one umbrella organisation.

However, despite the discrepancy, this was wonderful news to my ears. Phone calls were made, and my children were brought back home. Oh, how pleased I was! How relieved I was! I thanked God with every bit of my soul. I thanked Nik for getting me through it all. If I had continued drinking, who knows what would have happened, but he had the sense and control to stop me from making that mistake; a mistake that would have had devastating consequences. It was that Nik whom I had fallen in love with all those years ago. He pulled me through that awful situation. He was responsible for the mess but made amends when it mattered. I was still dealing with two different personalities; the good and the evil; still lingering and confusing my world. It was all leading me further and further into the centre of a whirlpool of bad blood and dark energy.

Of all people, I ended up going for comfort and ease to the very person responsible for the mess. I could not be alone. I would have gone delirious. I needed someone with me, even if it was Nik. I was wounded and vulnerable; and needed help.

ISR Report

LEICESTERSHIRE POLICE

26/05/2012 17:07:49	ODI, DUPLICATE/ UPDATE ON INC	LEP-260512-0607/LEP	TELEPHONE
Priority: (8) 8	DRUNK MOTHER LOST KIDS – DUP 607	CH07	Officer Dealing: 1387
Operator: 8583	Dispatcher:	CH07 (455952,304901)	Creator Wkstn: BC04

ADDRESS INFORMATION:

EAST GATE SCHOOL LEICESTER, LE3 6DN	Disposition code:
	DUPLICATE INCIDENT
Proximity:	
Complainant Information:	Theme:
NICOLETTE WALLACE	ADMINISTRATION
XXX NEW PARKS BOULEVARD LEICESTER LE3 9SA	
VICTIM [?] Media Consent [?] Feedback?	

Call Received: 17:07:49	26/05/2012

Incident Created	17:07:49
Address Validated	17:08:46
Incident confirmed	17:13:35
Transfer Sent	17:1346
Resource Dispatched	
Arrival at Scene	
Resource Cleared	
Incident Resulted	

CALL CARD – XREF CALL – LEP- 260512 – 0404 ASSOCIATED BY OPERATOR 1387

ISR Comments	
CALLER REPORTING THAT HER CHILDREN HAVE BEEN TAKEN BY SCHOOL	17:12:40
SHE ADMITS TO BEING DRUNK AT SCHOOL	17:12:51
INCIDENT RELATES	17:12:59
SHE WISHES TO SEE KIDS	17:13:07
2 X CHILDREN	17:13:21
INCIDENT NUMBER GIVEN	17:13:30
ADVISED THAT POLICE SHALL BE COMING TO ADDRESS TO ASSIST	17:14:17
CALLER SAYS HER DAUGHTER IS AUTISTIC SHE IS ANGEL 9YRS DOB 03/07/02	17:15:09

OTHER CHILD IS 5YRS OLD STAR DOB 16/01/2007	17:15:52
CALLER ADVISED CHILDREN TAKEN TO CARE OF POLICE AND SHALL SPEAK WITH HER AS SOON AS POSSIBLE	17:17:25
BEING DEALT WITH ON LINKED, D/G REQUESTED	17:22:33
SHE NEVER LOST THE CHILDREN – SHE LEFT HER KIDS AT THE SCHOOL	17:25:06
PC692 PREV ATTENDED – WILL ATTEND FEMALES ADDRESS TO ADVISE HER CHILDREN ARE NOW IN CARE OF S/SERVICES	17:25:36
HAVE TRIED RINGING THE FEMALE TWICE TO ADVISE HER TO REMAIN AT H/A AND AWAIT OFFICER – GOING TO V/MAIL, NO MESSAGE LEFT	17:27:03
FURTHER CALL FROM FEMALE ASKING ABOUT THE CHILDREN HAVE ADVISED THAT POLICE WILL ATTEND AND SEE HER PER ABOVE COMMENTS AND THAT SHE IS TO REMAIN AT THE ADDRESS	18:24:38
FOLLOW UP ACTIONS:	18:46:36
Result Code: 'ODI'	18:53:40
No. of Arrests N.F.A NO. OF Reports	18:53:40
Handling officer:1387	18:53:40
Qualifiers, none apply	18:53:40
LEP-260512-0607 HAS BEEN DISPOSED	18:53:40

CHAPTER 7

Great Yarmouth - July 2012.
The girls were excited. I was excited. My niece, Muni, was coming along too. We were all looking forward to a magnificent holiday. It was my birthday, and we had booked a seven-day holiday with Havens in Norfolk. We did our last-minute shopping and off to the coach we went. It was a beautiful journey, long but tolerable. We were playing games and just having fun. Everybody was in a holiday mood, and I was not getting any bother from Nik.

We got to our resort park and checked in then went in search of our caravan, which was conveniently located right at the centre of the park, next to the beach and rides. We had booked a three-bedroom camp. I was in one with Nik; Muni and Star shared the other and Angel was in by herself. She needed her own space and she had that. We unpacked and decided to head for the beach. The moment we got there, we heard a loud splash in the water. We looked back and there was Nik in the water daring everyone to dip. It was chilly and none of us had bathing suits. We had just gone to explore the beach, but my Nik got carried away and jumped in, clothes and all. It was funny; we had a laugh and he lost his glasses which he forgot to take off before he plunged in.

We walked around a little and then went to settle down ready for a busy day the following day.

" Let's watch a movie," Nik said.

"Sure, that sounds like a good idea. What should we watch?"

"The last king of Scotland," he suggested.

"No, it is not a suitable movie for us to watch with a teenager, she's too young." Nik you know there is a sex scene in it and I don't think it's appropriate. Besides, that is *our* movie. It's personal to us." Star was already settled in bed playing on her Nintendo and Angel was settled in her room on her laptop. I looked at the time and realised it was late, so I suggested she watches TV from her room in order to reserve energy for the following day. We chilled out on the sofa for a while drinking and watching a movie.

"Now, I need you to promise me that there will be no drinking until after we have spent the day with the girls doing whatever it is that they want. We are on holiday, I know, but we have to be responsible. After we put the girls to bed, we can drink as much as we want. Agreed?"

He shrugged. "Yeah, I know we talked about it already."

"I know, I am saying it again because it is important to the girls and me. I know it's my birthday, but the holiday is really for them. We woke up feeling fresh the next morning. I made breakfast whilst the girls showered and got ready for the day. After I had cleared up after breakfast, I went to have a shower and when I came out, I saw Nik in the kitchen downing a three-litre bottle of White Lightning cider. I was so annoyed I stormed towards him and wrestled with him for the bottle. Through the scuffle I managed to pour the whole lot down the sink. Big mistake. There was alcohol all over the place. Fortunately, Star and Muni were outside when this altercation occurred, and Angel was in her room, but they came in when they heard the noise.

I had cider on myself, in my hair, on the floor, everywhere and I had to clean up the mess. I was so angry with Nik and felt really let down. He had promised me. It was only for a few hours that I asked him not to drink. I was hurt even more by the fact that he got physical with me whilst I tried to get rid of the alcohol. I told the girls that it was all right, and I decided to take a walk with them to the local shops to see what we needed for the beach that afternoon. We left Nik at the camp. I needed time apart from him. I was still very upset, but felt better by the time we got back. We were all ready for the beach.

"Okay girls get your swimming costumes, towels and flip-flops out. Let's get ready to have fun with the waves!

"Yeeeaaaah!" we screamed with joy. There was one problem: all our clothes were missing. Nik was slumped on the sofa, clearly wasted. He must have had more to drink when we left him, and it was clear that he had hidden our clothes. I woke him up and demanded our clothes back.

"I don't know what you're talking about." He said as he turned away.

"Motherfucker-! You are not going to spoil my children's holiday. I spent a lot of money on this trip. You said you were willing to come with us and that you were going to behave yourself. And now you are hiding my children's clothes to stop them from having fun.?" I was seething with rage. I went outside and looked at the trailer's sides, inside the wheels, cupboards, under the sink. Nothing. No clothes. Then I saw him downing another bottle of cider. I charged forwards and almost jumped on him. We wrestled, and he pushed me against the wall, but I was not budging.

After minutes of scuffling, and my head being bashed everywhere, I managed to run outside and rang the police. The house was a mess. He was still around and was arrested at the scene in Great Yarmouth, just less than twenty-four hours into our holiday. After the police had left, more policemen came to evict us from the resort park, even though they had taken Nik away. They saw that I had three children, but they still evicted us. I was devastated. I was broken. Words cannot begin to describe what I felt at that moment. I had spent over £1000.00 of my money on this holiday. He did not contribute a penny. The alcohol that he was fighting me for, had been bought with my money. The beach clothes he wore, were bought with my money and that was all I got in return?

I tried pleading with them, told them the circumstances, but they would not hear me. Apparently, he was still hanging about the entrance, so we all had to leave.

"AAAAAAAAAAAAAAGGGGGHHHHHHHH!" I screamed at the top of my lungs. We began packing. We had fresh food in the fridge, plus all the beach gadgets we had bought the previous day. My mind was racing, and I was filled with rage and heartbreak. We were escorted to the gates of the park, and there I stood, stuck. What was I going to do? I looked at the three girls and my heart was pierced. *What had I done? Why had I allowed Nik to spoil my children's holiday? How could I be so stupid and selfish?* I had given him a chance even though I knew he could not be trusted. But I guess deep down I gave him that chance so that he could prove himself. I thought if we were to go away from our everyday life, the situation would change. Obviously, I was wrong. I had put my children in a risky situation. We were homeless and miles away from home. I could not hold back my tears. I always avoided breaking down in front of the kids, but my tears could not be stopped now. My niece tried to console me and that made me feel worse.

I had to think fast, I had to forget about the money I had already wasted and devise a new plan. I looked at my girls again and I thought to myself that I was not going to let that jerk take so much that away from my daughters. I hailed a taxi.

"Can you please help us find a B&B, something not too expensive but family-friendly?" I asked the driver.

After a couple of minutes, we pulled up in front of a row of B&B's and we managed to find a family room at £20 a night. We had our own food, so the owner directed the manager to cook breakfast in the mornings, and I paid for six nights. It was not as planned, but we had a wonderful time. We were only a few yards from the beach, and we would spend all our days there, having a blast, going on rides and shopping. I had done a bank transaction to withdraw money from the children's savings account. It did not matter; my children had the holiday they were meant to have. The owner was very kind to us. He would drive us around some afternoons when he was free or drop us at a different park and pick us up later. It turned out to be a blessing after all, and for those seven days we were there, I tried not to think about Nik.

When we finally arrived home after hours of travel, there was a knock at the door. I opened it and saw Marnie standing outside.

"Marnie, hi, how are you?" I said, excited to see him and giving him a hug.

"I'm good thanks_" he began, but I cut him off before he could go any further.

"Do you know what your friend did to us in Great Yarmouth?" I said, still standing in the hallway.

"Yeah, that's kinda why I am here", he said in a low voice.

"What do you mean?"

"He is outside He wants to see you."

"You'd better be kidding me!" I exclaimed in disgust. I then narrated everything that had gone on and expressed my resentments about Nik's behaviour and character. Marnie left but was back within minutes, begging on his friend's behalf. I thought to myself. *He must really be embarrassed if he cannot face me at the house. Usually, he would have come for a confrontation for having him kicked out of the caravan.* Frankly, deep down I was scared of how he was going to react because he had no money to travel back, nor to secure accommodation. At that time, however, I did not much care because of the loathing that was going on inside me.

Eventually, I agreed to walk to the car, parked around the corner, with Marnie. The moment Nik saw me he got out of the car and Marnie went to sit in the driver's seat. Nik pleaded with me many times and told me how sorry he was and how he had been stuck and had to be saved by a stranger. Although he was apologising, he was trying to minimise his role as much as possible so that he did not take all the blame.

"You're an asshole!" I shouted and turned to walk away. He called behind me, but I did not listen. The social worker heard about this incident from the police report, and when

I was confronted, I told him about the events. It was then, that he made me sign a formal agreement, that I was not to let Nikolas Martins anywhere near my children or me. He was no longer permitted to be anywhere near our property, and I was to report to the police each time he turned up, failure to do so would lead to procedures against my children.

~ ~ ~

Even though the protective order was still in place, Nik would still call and occasionally I would meet up with him in a park somewhere away from the children and the house. If I refused to meet him he would threaten to come to the house because. He would tell me how much he missed me and how much he needed see me. And there were a few occasions when that would happen at times, I did not need to refuse, he would just turn up and tell me he did not have credit to call. For example, there was one incident when the social worker turned up unannounced and caught Nik hiding in the closet.

I had heard the knock at the door, and I looked out through the window and saw him standing there. My heart lost a bit, I directed Nik to go upstairs and hide in my wardrobe and not make a sound. I let the social worker in and halfway through our conversation we had a sound upstairs. When he asked me whether there was someone upstairs, I denied it.

"Mind if I take a look?" I gestured with my hands and led him upstairs, hoping and praying for the best. But I knew the game was up, he opened the closet door and there he was. It was noted in the social services' reports and I was reminded of it at each meeting.

Since Nik was no longer a dominant part of my life, Nina and I decided to go back to our old tradition where she would bring Marie over for the weekend and we would chill and watch movies. Everything was going well until I received a phone call.

"Who's there with you?" he demanded to know.

"It's Nina and Marie, they are spending the weekend."

"Okay I am coming over," he said.

"No, no, no, we were planning on having just a girls' night," I answered.

Just as I said that sentence, I heard Nina on her phone.

"I thought you said it was just Nina and the kids?" he quizzed.

"Yes, it is just us," I said trying to convince him.

"So why do I hear Nina speaking to someone else in the background? Are you lying to me?" He was getting agitated, and I had to try and take control. I did not want to give him any reason to come to the house. Social services were on my tail; the neighbours had had enough of his menacing behaviour and the children had seen enough.

"Listen, why don't I come over there instead, huh? We can chill without the children just you and me; I will ask Nina to look after them." I managed to convince him, so I explained everything to Nina and off I went to Upperton Road, Leicester, where he shared a space with one other guy. It was NASS accommodation, so they shared a living room, bathroom, and kitchen but he had his own bedroom. He had nothing in his bedroom apart from a bed, wardrobe, desk, and chair. There was no TV and no radio. On my way to his apartment, I stopped by the off-licence and bought two bottles of wine, I knew I would need them. That was the only way I could tolerate him; by being drunk myself.

When I arrived, I found him sitting in the living room with his roommate Steed, having a drink and conversation. I had brought some food for him, so I proceeded to put the ramekin in the fridge and came back to join them. Everything was going smoothly, and we were laughing and joking when there was a knock at the door. Steed went to open it and when he returned, he was followed by four other guys. The room was getting smaller. About half an hour later we were joined by two more guys and I was getting uncomfortable.

I did not know these people and therefore did not relate to their conversation. I asked Nik if we should excuse ourselves and spend time in his room, but he kept putting it off. Soon more guys came, and it was getting rowdy so I left and went to Nik's bedroom thinking he would be right behind me. I waited by myself for an hour then I went to get him. He refused and asked for a few more moments. I went back and continued drinking. I was angry and frustrated. He had rung when I was at home chilling, and I was only in this situation because of his persistent demand to be with me. Now that he had captured me. He knew where I was, so he did not worry any more. But he did not care enough to think that he had left me in a room for hours on my own.

I had made myself comfortable, so after three hours I got up from the bed and began to get myself ready to leave. There was no point being there, he was entertaining guests. I needed to use the toilet first and as I passed through, he spotted me and noticed that I was fully clothed, including my shoes. He came charging over.

"What do you think you are doing!" he shouted grabbing me by my arm.

"What does it look like? I am going home Nik! I have been stuck in that little room all by myself for three hours with no entertainment what-so-ever. Oh no, you don't get to do that. I'm off!" I shouted. Our argument was drowned by the boys talking at the top of their voices. We carried on into the bedroom where I reached for my handbag ready to leave. I stepped forward but he was blocking the door, I tried to get out, but I was shoved so hard on to the bed, I bounced a bit on the mattress. I got up and was shoved down again. It happened about four times then I yelled out, "STOP IT! LET ME GO!"

I will never forget that incident for as long as I live. After screaming out, I unleashed the devil in him. His face darkened and his eyes opened as wide as if he had been possessed. He shoved me on the bed, jumped on top of me and put his elbow against my trachea.

"Today I will show you exactly how brutal I can be, bitch!"

He said these words with a frightening expression. His face was right into mine; our noses were almost touching. I could feel the weight of his body on top of me but most terrifying was the pressure he was applying to my throat. I couldn't breathe and I could not yell out; all my air was trapped. I was trying to wrestle with him, but I had no chance. I was no longer fighting with Nik, but some demonic spirit that had overtaken him. I could see things starting to go hazy and blurry, and I saw the images of my girls. It was then that I managed to release a little bit of pressure enough to yell "Help!" which did not quite come out as the word but rather as a bellowing sound. Thank goodness someone must have been walking to the kitchen because the door burst open.

Several of them managed to pull him off me and restrained him. I was petrified and shaking visibly. Of all the attacks, this was the most personal, in terms of contact. He was on top of me choking me, and he could see I was about to pass out, but he continued his deadly grip on my throat. What if those guys were not there that day? Would I have lived another day to see my children? One of the guys had a car and offered to drive me home, but I knew better. I rang for a taxi and was determined not to tell Nina, my best friend, what had happened. Again, I pretended that I'd had a marvellous time, but inside I was rotten to the core. The pain was eating me up like a disease. I had no one to turn to.

Nina had told me many times to leave him. Many people had told me, even family, but nobody knew how difficult it was. One does not just walk away from a person who displays psychotic behaviour. Such people do not live by our rules. They make up their own rules as they go along and make sure to enforce and control victims. At that time, I did consider myself a victim. I was a battered woman and considered a bad mother according to social services reports.

I loved my children with all my heart and there was no way I would have wanted a life like that for them. Domestic violence affects everyone in the vicinity, and I knew it was not healthy for my children. I blamed myself often, for not being strong enough. For not being whole, when I met Nik Perhaps, I expected him to do too much. Perhaps my best intentions were misguided, but I offered nothing but love and loyalty. I fed him and gave him somewhere to lay his head and his gratitude was another fresh wound.

It was not the first time he had used a choke hold on me. During the summer holidays I always had my thirteen-year-old niece around. After one such break, it was time for her to return home after a two-week vacation with the girls and her mother was coming to fetch her from Birmingham -.and she had decided to spend the weekend at my house before leaving for Birmingham. I took advantage to take some 'me' time by asking my sister-in-law to take care of the girls, whilst I went to Derby to see Nik. He had been over to see me a week before, and all had gone well. He had got on with my niece and we had played happy families. Now I wanted time with just him alone, without the children, something we both agreed, so I set off for Derby.

When I arrived, he was waiting for me at the coach stop, and we walked to his house, passing through the off-licence for some food and alcohol. I knew he never had food in his house, and I often wondered how he survived. Everything was going so well, we laughed, danced and made love. I did not worry about the children because I knew they were in safe hands, although I would phone and check in here and there. Next morning, from the moment we woke up we continued drinking without a care in the world. I was having fun until his roommate came home. I heard the front door open and shut and Nik explained to me that his roommate often slept at his sister's house, and that was where he had been.

Moments later, I jumped out of bed and reached for my dressing gown.

"Where are you going?" he asked abruptly.

"I am going to use the toilet," I answered, him zipping up.

"Oh no, you're not!" he said, jumping out of bed and grabbing me by my arm. I was taken aback.

"What do you mean? I can't use the toilet?" I asked in confusion.

"You just want to go out there and check my roommate out. Why all of a sudden do you now have an urge to use the toilet-? You were lying down with me just now, and you never mentioned needing the toilet".

"Seriously?!" I could not believe what was coming out of his mouth, nor how he came up with these dots, managed to connect them and make something meaningful in his head. We struggled and argued. I managed to push passed him, then went to the bathroom and locked the door. He was kicking and shouting all sorts of obscenities. It was then that I decided it was time I went home to get away from a heated situation

.

I unlocked the door and went to the kitchen; he was right behind me. He was still shouting but I ignored him, which made him furious. He pinned me against the living room wall with his hand on my throat while applying pressure. I shouted for help and his roommate came running, but he was told it was none of his business and if he knew what was good for him, he'd go back into his room. He obliged. Nik then dragged me by the throat into the bedroom and threw me onto the bed. He continued shouting, telling me what a slut I was. For a moment he left the room, so I took that chance to make my move. I started getting dressed quickly, grabbed my bag and I met him at the bedroom entrance.

"Bitch you wanna fuck with me! I will show you that you can't fuck with me!" He put his drink on the floor and swooped me up in his arms, carried me to the bed and threw me on it. He began unzipping my boots and taking them off whilst at the same time preventing me from getting up.

"Today I am going to show you a different type of regime and discipline. You have heard about the Mugabe regime? They beat you up under the soles of your feet because that is the only part that doesn't leave scars".

Both my boots were thrown on the floor and my socks were stripped off. I began to receive the Mugabe corporal punishment. Nik used his hands and fists, then he switched to his belt. It hurt, I watched him as he administered each and every lash. This was the man who declared his deep love for me, the man who said he never wanted to lose me. The same man was hurting me beyond imagination.

I lay there hopeless and helpless. I needed it to stop. I wanted him to stop being cruel to me. Yes, he did stop it for a while when he apologised and made sweet love to me. It was then, that I knew he was sorry, truly sorry. My soul had spoken to his soul. He was not an evil person, just possessed by evil. I wanted to help him, but he was making it so difficult. My love for him faded each time he hurt me. I did not call the police; I did not want to involve the police because they had a duty to inform social services. So, for as long as there were no potential witnesses, my secret was safe. I stayed an extra night, then left for Leicester the following morning. My feet hurt, but all I needed were comfortable shoes and no one would ever find out.

****

CB/01001/13-5 Summary	CRIME/Incident 19/02/2013

Offence Details   **PUBLIC ORDER**

Times / Days/ Dates **1900 Tuesday 10/02/2013**
HO Code: 06639

Offence location: **xxx NEW PARKS BOULEVARD**
LEICESTER, LE3 9SA

Aggrieved: **MISS NICOLETTE WALLACE, XXX**
                            NPB, LEICESTER, LE3 9SA

Repeat victim: **YES**   *Support required*: **YES**

Reporting Details: When: **19/02/2013**
How: TO POLICE PATROL
Where: CONTROL ROOM

Reporting Officer: **CONSTABLE 1522 BYRONE**

Person Reporting: **MISS NICOLETTE WALLACE,**
XXX NPB, LEICESTER, LE3 9SA
Phone Numbers: xxxxxxxxxx

HOME

Premises: **DWELLING SEMI**
Site: **URBAN RESIDENTIAL**
Level:
Incident Type: **Domestic incident (repeat victim)**
Child at risk referral to social
services; body camera not at scene
Domestic incident medium risk

Summary **Medium risk domestic – ex partner**
attends location and begins
arguing with aggrieved, during
verbal altercation d/p pushes
aggrieved over at which she stands
on glass causing deep laceration to
the sole of her foot.

Suspects: **NIKOLAS MARTINS, African**
Caribbean
Male D.O.B; 26/01/1978
Age: 35 short black hair
Clothes: jacket, jumper, jeans
Brown eyes

*********INFORMATION / INTELLIGENCE*******

During the course of the evening on Tuesday the 19th of February 2013, the ambulance was called to the premises of xxx New Parks Boulevard Leicester following a 999 call. The ambulance service reference number for the call is 5341752. CAS control were informed that the caller was a six-year-old child who stated that her "mother was drunk" and that she was in the house with her ten-year old autistic sister.

When CAS responder 6042 arrived at the address the door was answered by a female child. She began to tell him that she was in the address with her mother who was drunk, but in the event her mother (the detainee Nicolette Wallace) then came down the stairs and prevented the child from saying anything else. CAS 6042 noted that Nicolette had an injury to the sole of her right foot that was bleeding to a marked degree. He quickly realised that she was intoxicated which raised concern in respect of the welfare of the children present. Nicolette refused any treatment.

6042 then contacted CAS control who in turn contacted the police. He then saw two children leave number xxx in turn walk down the road a short distance (it transpired to number xxx) followed by Nicolette herself. Shortly thereafter PC's 2110, 1522 and PCSO 4065 arrived at scene. Having done so the officers first liaised with the CAS responder before then noticing that the co-detainee, Nicolette's partner Nikolas Martins was standing further up the road outside number xxx. He was spoken to and found to be heavily intoxicated, was wearing a brown bloodstained timberland boot on his right foot (he was barefoot on the left) and was in possession of a set of keys, one of which appeared to be a house key that was snapped in two. The other half to said house keys was found in the outside of the door lock to number xxx.

Nicolette then also came out onto the street from number xxx and was spoken to by officers. She was extremely intoxicated, verbally abusive, and non-compliant. It was noted that she was bleeding heavily from a wound to her right foot (she was barefoot) and appeared to be wearing Nikolas's other timberland boot on her left foot. Between being abusive she stated to PC 1522 that Nikolas had arrived at her address drunk, there had been an argument relating to some papers that had been served today (we do not know what these were but we believe they may have related to a non-molestation order) as a consequence of which he had pushed her, she had stepped back and stood on a glass which duly smashed and caused the injury.

Nikolas was duly arrested on suspicion of assault ABH. It had initially been the intention to facilitate medical intervention with Nicolette at the scene, and indeed the CAS responder managed to apply a bandage. (the offence being borne out when she left her home address with her children).

Having viewed the inside of number xxx New Parks Boulevard it is evident that the injury to Nicolette occurred within the living room of the address. There was a small pile of glass on the floor near to the settee with a blood stained tissue nearby. It appears Nicolette then went upstairs and tried to clean the wound in the bathroom where more blood was found on the floor. Numerous bloodstains matching the nature of injury were also found inside number xxx New Parks Boulevard where she had walked around within that address.

Her two children are listed as xxxxxxx DOB xxxxxxx and XXXXX xxxxxx DOB xxxx They were located at xxxxxx, the home address of xxxxxx. This individual was spoken to and was also in drink, albeit she was completely compos mentos and showing no signs of intoxication. The decision was therefore taken (with her agreement) to leave the children at her address for the night.

*************THREATS AND RISKS*************

On the strength of this incident Nicolette can be verbally abusive and very obstructive when intoxicated. This by definition increases her vulnerability at the hands of Nikolas. The most vulnerable persons by far in the equation however are her children, the older of which is autistic. The fact that Nicolette chooses to drink to excess whilst in charge of her children is demonstrable evidence of her lack of understanding or responsibility in respect of this issue

Interim Report Submitted By: PC2110

The police report is quite detailed. It was the day after Nik had been served with the molestation order. I had filed against him in court with the advice from my solicitor, after he kept forcing entry to the house. That order had been granted in July the previous year, but had not been able to serve him due to him having no fixed abode. He was moving from one place to the next, exhausting all avenues and causing mayhem along the way. They managed to locate him in February the following year at a friend's house. He had been calling me numerous times, on that day but I was ignoring him. But I knew the consequences of that, he would end up at my front door making trouble. I was not aware that he had been served, I just thought he was going through his moments of bullying and control. I later learnt that there was a scuffle at his mate's house and police were called and realised there was an order against him. It had taken them seven months to finally serve him with the order.

Eventually, I answered his call, he began to recite the order to me. He was cursing and furious, and I was very afraid. You see, when my solicitor advised me to make a molestation application, she forgot to tell me that my statement against the perpetrator would be attached to the application. So Nik had in his possession a statement that I had submitted to the court, with all the incidents and all I thought of him. That was a dangerous situation, which, had I known about it previously, I would never have agreed to.

I went knocking at Seth and Mika's for help. I knew they could not do much, but I asked them to keep an eye out if they saw Nik in the area. They had become people I turned to for protection, despite their drinking. I remember an incident when Nik turned up and managed to gain access to the house. I asked him to leave, and he refused, so I left with the children. We went to sit with Seth and Mika for about an hour and then decided to go back home. I thought he would have been tired of waiting for us and had maybe left the scene.

When we arrived home, the front door was locked. He had locked us out. I banged and shouted but to no avail. I knocked at my neighbour's house to see if he could break the door down, but also failed.

"Go back where you came from!" I heard Nik shout back. I was astounded, I had been locked out of my own home by someone who did not even have the right to be at the property. Everything seemed so insane and so unreal. I did not understand a thing that was happening in my life, and felt so guilty about putting my children through it all. They deserved better. I was ruining their lives and corrupting their innocent minds.

We went back to Seth and Mika's, and I told them what was going on. This time they were joined by their other friend, Alberto, with whom Nik had previously accused me of having an affair with. He said that was the only reason why I hung out with them was that I liked Alberto. They managed to break into the house through the bathroom window and a brawl broke out. They wrestled Nik outside and he was shouting all sorts of obscenities to me. All this went on as the children watched. It was breaking my heart.

However, on this precise day of the police incident report, they offered to sit with me at the house in case he showed up. They were drinking and I was drinking. The phone calls continued to come in and I continued to ignore them. I knew it wouldn't be long before he came. The waiting game made me more anxious, so I was drinking quite a lot on that day. The waiting game was over, he finally came to confront me with the order.

I tried to reason with him, telling him that I had been forced to file a restraining order and that if I had not, the social services would take my children. I told him that all the things contained in my statement were words of my social worker and solicitor.

"Sweetheart, I knew you would get the statement, c'mon. I thought you would know that it was not me who was responsible for all those things that were said about you," I lied. Mika and Seth engaged him in conversation for a while and then things got messy. Nik pushed me so hard, that I knocked a glass off the table and stepped on it before landing on the floor. There was blood everywhere, and I had a deep gash on the sole of my right foot.

Mika looked at it and suggested I needed to go to the hospital to get it stitched up, but I refused. I went upstairs to try and clean it up, but the blood was just flowing. The argument continued, Seth was fighting Nik and there was commotion everywhere, so I asked them to leave. But Nik stayed. We started arguing again and he was accusing me of having an affair with Alberto, then it all got out of hand. I really believe he was not going to stop hurting me. Here I was bleeding from an injury yet he was still aggressive towards me.

"Star, call 999, call the police!" I screamed to my daughter who was five years old at the time not six as the police report stated. The medic came and told me that he was ringing an ambulance and the police because he believed that I had been drinking. I was so scared at the mention of the police, so I called to both children and asked them to walk to Mika's house, which was four doors away. I got myself together and, I put Nik's Timberland boot on my good foot and rushed to Mika's. I was right behind the children and my foot was making a trail of blood.

When the police arrived I was angry, anxious, frightened, confused and all sorts of thoughts were going on in my head. They suggested I go in the ambulance, but I refused because I did not want to leave my children. They had gone through enough. I explained to the police, that I was angry because no one told me that Nik would read my statement in the molestation order. However, they kept pressing me to go to the hospital, which I kept refusing to do and I was getting more and more worn out by the situation. They had Nik, they had seen my injuries, and did not wish to give a statement nor go to the hospital. I just wanted them to go and leave us in peace

.

But they turned against me and arrested me for being drunk and disorderly. They even added an extra charge of being drunk with children in a public place, even though I was not physically with the children as they had walked to Mika's house. I watched them walk to Mika's gate from my gate and then I proceeded behind them. The same people who had been called to help me as a victim were the same people putting me in the back of a police van and treating me like a criminal. To this day I have a big scar across the sole of my foot, a brutal reminder of the savage attack and the unjust system.

Words cannot describe how I felt at that moment as they drove me to the police station. Unless one's lived through it, it is very difficult to explain. The devastation was unimaginable and yet again I felt let down by the system. There was no way out for me. To me they were all tormenters, except, Nik was a better tormenter. He apologised and made love to me and sometimes that made the pain go away.

~ ~ ~

ISR Report

LEICESTERSHIRE POLICE

28/07/2012 3 01:16:23	PQA, CONCERN FOR SAFETY	LEP-280713-0056/LEP	999
Priority: (2) Priority	BANGING AT DOOR	CB01	Officer Dealing : 2912
Operator: 8882	Dispatcher : 0510	CB01 (655534,786490)	Creator Wkstn: BC13

ADDRESS INFORMATION:

XXX NEW PARKS BOULEVARD LEICESTER, LE3 9SA	Disposition code:
	SUSPICIOUS CIRCUMSTANCES
Proximity:	
Complainant Information:	Theme:
NICOLETTE WALLACE	PUBLIC SAFETY

XXX NEW PARKS BOULEVARD LEICESTER LE3 9SA	
VICTIM [?] Media Consent [?] Feedback?	

Call Received: 01:16:23	28/07/2013
Incident Created	01:16:23
Address Validated	01;17:10
Incident confirmed	01:17:34
Transfer Sent	01:17:35
Resource Dispatched	01:20:41
Arrival At Scene	01:27:15
Resource Cleared	03:26:36
Incident Resulted	
ISR Comments	
CALLER HAS SOMEBODY BANGING ON DOOR	01:16:44
SHE SAYS THEY KEEP WALKING AWAY AND COMING BACK	01:16:54
CALLER STATES THERE IS A POLICE MARKER ON HER ADDRESS	01:17:43
BUT HAVE LOOKED ON SYSTEM AND CANNOT SEE ONE	01:17:55
CALLER SAYS IT COULD BE AN EX PARTNER, THOUGH SHE THINKS HE IS IN HOSPITAL AT THE MOMENT	01:18:07
EX PARTNER IS NIKOLAS MARTINS	01:18:28
ALSO AT ADDRESS IS CALLER'S 2 CHILDREN	01:18:47

NIKOLAS DOB 26/01/1978	01:19:45
BUT CALLER DOES NOT KNOW IF IT IS HIM, SHE IS TOO SCARED TO OPEN THE DOOR	01:19:54
SHE ASKED FOR OFFICERS TO COME QUICKLY, SHE WAS SCARED	01:20:09
THE PERSON IS AT HER DOOR NOW	01:20:15
NOTHING TO SUGGEST VULNERABILITY, THOUGH CHILDREN AT ADDRESS	01:20:39
NOT A REPEAT VICTIM	01:20:58
CR13 JUST HEARD SOME KNOCKING, NOT SEEN ANYONE	01:35:02
CR21 COULDN'T CONFIRM IF OUR MALE WAS RESPONSIBLE FOR DOOR KNOCK	01:53:27
NO OFFENCES HAVING CHECKED THE MALE ON PNC THERE ARE NO CONDITIONS WILL TAKE HIM TO ST PETER'S ROAD	01:53:54
CHECKED OUT NIKOLAS MARTINS – NO RESTRICTIONS ON HIM. TAKING HIM TO ST PETERS	01:54:15
LIAISED WITH IMMIGRATION RE THIS MALE- INSTRUCTED TO ARREST HIM TO BE DEALT BY IMMIGRATION	02:12:30
4447/2317 ATTENDANCE UPDATE 01/08/2013	09:28:59
I ATTENDED AND SPOKE TO THE CALLER, SHE STATED THAT SHE HAD HEARD SOMEONE KNOCKING ON THE DOOR AND GUESSED IT WAS HER EX PARTNER,	10:40:29

SHE DID NOT SEE OR SPEAK TO HIM SHE JUST CALLED THE POLICE THEREFORE THERE IS NO D/T AND NO NEED FOR ANY FORMS	
RECEIVED A CALL FROM ADRIAN TAYLOR – SOCIAL WORKER FOR THE CHILDREN AT THIS ADDRESS- HE WANTED TO SPEAK TO OFFICER THAT DEALT. HE THEN WANTED TO KNOW WHY HE HAD NOT BEEN INFORMED OF THIS INCIDENT. I HAVE INFORMED HIM THAT THE INC DID NOT INVOLVE CHILDREN AND WAS A CALL REGARDING SOMEONE KNOCKING AT THE DOOR.	15:22:36
HE THEN PROVIDED THE NAME OF THE MALE TO ME AND SAID THAT THIS CALLER HAS INFORMED HIM THAT THE MALE HAD BEEN ARRESTED FOR ASSAULT	15:24:16
CALL RECEIVED FROM ADRIAN TAYLOR IN CAIU. I HAVE SHARED THE NECESSARY INFORMATION WITH HIM ABOUT THE INCIDENT TO ENABLE HIM TO UNDERSTAND THAT THIS IS NOT A SAFEGUARDING ISSUE. ADAM WANTED MORE INFO RELATING TO OTHER INCIDENTS AT THE ADDRESS. HE WAS ADVISED HE SHOULD GO THROUGH THE FORMAL CHANNELS OF A STRAT MEETING TO OBTAIN THESE DETAILS	16:00:32

Dates were important to Nik; birthdays, Valentines' Day and Christmas especially. Those were the dates I was sure he would turn up. Although on this particular day of the police incident report, I did not think he would because he had been sectioned the day before.

I had received a call from one of the doctors in the psychiatric unit, since Nik had listed me as his next of kin. Nik was apparently found on the street the night before in the middle of the road, He had no shirt on and was shouting and yelling. The doctor advised me that Nik had been picked up again a few days prior. He then handed me the phone to speak to him because Nik was insisting.

He was not making much sense when I spoke to him. He told me how he was arrested a few days before and that I had visited him in his cell with another man and then left him there. At that point, I feared for him, I really wished there was a way I could get him out of the dark hole he was in. The man was living in total darkness, and it pained me to watch him waste away. He was handsome and intelligent, but this demon had completely taken him over .

It was Nik knocking at my door. He had removed his tubes and escaped from the hospital then made his way straight to me. Although the police did not find him, he must have been watching them, and when it was all clear, he made his move. I was stupid enough not to ask who was at the door, I assumed it was the police, but once that door was opened, Nik was in. I asked him to leave and to go back to the hospital because I could see clearly that he was in a mess.

An argument broke out and he picked up the saucepan that had water in it and whacked me in the face with it. Immediately I saw blood pouring from my face onto my clothes.

"Oh my God, what have you done?!" I screamed at him. I was wet from the water and so was the floor. Fortunately, the water was cold. When I had heard a knock at the door I was just about to boil some eggs and had not turned the gas on. I sustained a deep cut on my right eye and some swelling which again I managed to hide well with my wig and makeup. I did not report these injuries to the police and to this day, I have a permanent scar across my right eyebrow.

There had been a police marker on the address for months, yet failed to identify it. The marker meant that any 999 calls from the address should be responded to in minutes and in my case because of the amount of violence that was going on. Yet the police report even goes on to state: *"There are no restrictions on him"*…*"nothing to suggest vulnerability"* and *"not a repeat victim"*—all this while the social services held a file on him. It was not the first time the police marker was missed, and no appropriate action taken.

After this incident, I was very concerned about him. I rang his mother and invited her to come and sort him out. He was homeless and moving from house to house and at times sleeping outside and going for days without food. Because of the restrictions we had from social services, I could no longer accommodate him, and his behaviour had become unpredictable, so I was not willing to risk my children. But even though he was not permitted at my premises, I arranged for his mother to meet him at my house. He feared and respected his mother, and I was confident he would not hurt me in her presence. She was travelling from London and was going to be spending the night at my house, and so was he. I was willing to take that risk; it was the only way I thought I could help save him; through his mother.

Because it was sports day at Angel's school, I arranged for Joan to drive Nik to the train station to pick her up then take them to my house, where I would join them later. I was a bit nervous about meeting Nik's mother. We had created a good relationship over the telephone, but I had never met her in person. When I walked into the lounge with the children, she was seated on the two-seater opposite her son, who sat on the three-seater. She looked really glamorous and had some of Nik's features. She was quite a big woman, but proportionally shaped with curvy hips. I went up to her to give her a hug, then sat next to Nik. We exchanged greetings, and I apologised for not picking her up at the train station. She was smartly dressed and well-groomed. I felt that it was a good thing I had been away because it gave them a chance to talk in private.

I cooked dinner, and we all sat around the table and feasted. I then took out some Bailey's Cream liqueur we had bought for her earlier. Nik said it was her favourite, but she turned it down saying she had quit drinking. She asked me if I could help her undo her braids since she never had the chance to do it earlier. It was a pleasure. I felt really close to her as if she were my own mother. Angel was helping too. We were bonding, and I enjoyed every minute of it.

After putting the girls to sleep, I prepared my bedroom ready for his mum. Nik and I were sleeping downstairs in the lounge on the floor. We all stayed up until late, then I helped her upstairs. She had just had hip surgery a few weeks back and was having trouble walking. I opened my desk drawer and took out some hospital documents I had been keeping to show her. I handed them to her for her perusal. They were self-explanatory. Nik had been sectioned on two occasions in one month because of his mental health and his abuse of alcohol. I told her about the fits that he had recently started to experience as well. Although I had never witnessed them in person, I had been told about them by his roommates at that time, who had come to me begging me to take him in, saying they could not help him anymore. But I refused to put myself through that horror again. I wanted his mother to know the seriousness of the situation. I had not just invited her to travel a six-hour journey for nothing; her son needed help, and I no longer had the capacity to give it to him. It had become a job for a mother to take care of. It was either that or the dungeon. I also showed her my cracked window which had been damaged by Nik, two weeks prior to her visit, by throwing a brick at it.

Next morning after the school run, I made us a nice English breakfast. As we sat at the table, she began telling Nik how disappointed she was that he was not doing anything with his life. She was saddened by the fact that he was unable to look after his own son. Then she began to cry. I felt sorry for her as a mother. It was not a good feeling to watch your child in distress or go through turmoil. She expressed how sorry she was for not being able to take him back to London with her because of her accommodation. She said she rented only a small room suitable for one person.

His mother then stated that she was going to make arrangements for him to return home, back to Africa, where they owned a big house. At least there she would feel at ease knowing he had a roof over his head and food in his stomach. She wanted me to help her find out from the home office about the process of voluntary return. She explained that in the meantime, she was going to arrange for his passport and birth certificate to be sent over. She was worried about how he had lost weight and the fact that he was homeless. Her pain was visible each time she looked at Nik. He sat next to his mother, listening attentively and nodding to everything she was saying. I stood up and went to the kitchen, where he followed me.

"Does she really think I could go all the way to Africa and leave you here by yourself?" he said, with a smirk on his face. I turned to him and asked why he was going along with her if he knew he did not want to return home. He said it was the only way to shut her up. I tried telling him not to lead her on in case getting the documents required spending cash.

He grinned at me and put his arms around me, kissed my forehead and said to me, as he held my face in his hands, "I am not leaving you, Nicolette; you are my wife. You just don't know it yet. Nicolette, you were given to me by God himself."

Then we kissed; he knew each and every button that controlled each part of my body and mind.

"Nicolette, I am going to ask you to please look after my son for me, make sure he has a place to sleep and food to eat." Those were his mother's words to me before she left. I felt for her having to go back to London without seeing where her son was going to lay his head that night or what he was going to eat before sleep. She seemed to have missed the whole point of why I had invited her to come over in the first place. But I said to myself, *"It is what it is."* At least I tried.

After she left, she sent me a text message thanking me for the nice hospitality and told me how comfortable she felt in my home. She also told me how much she appreciated me for helping and supporting Nik and even ended with the words 'I love you.'

Next time Nik's mom rang to talk about the issue of applying for the voluntary return, I told her that Nik was not interested in returning home. She swore that the last time she had spoken to him he was up for it, insisting that he would never lie to her. That was the last I heard of the matter. Since her departure, the situation became more desperate for him. Social services were watching me like a hawk and all his friends had shut their doors on him. He was in dire straits, and there was nothing much I could do but to watch and hurt. I hurt for him because I loved him. I hurt for him because I felt that his own family had abandoned him. I hurt for him because he had become homeless and all alone. I hurt for him because he was no longer a pretty sight.

ISR Report

LEICESTERSHIRE POLICE

04/08/2013 09:28:46	ASB, ANTI SOCIAL BEHAVIOUR	LEP-040813-0286LEP	999
Priority: (2) Priority	ASSAULTED BY BOYFRIEND	CB01	Officer Dealing : 4447
Operator: 0381	Dispatcher: 3770	CB01 (000000,786490)	Creator Wkstn: BC02

ADDRESS INFORMATION:

XXX NEW PARKS BOULEVARD LEICESTER, LE3 9SA	Disposition code:
	VIOLENCE AND PUBLIC ORDER
Proximity:	
Complainant Information:	Theme:
NICOLETTE WALLACE	CRIME
XXX NEW PARKS BOULEVARD LEICESTER LE3 9SA	
VICTIM [?] Media Consent [?] Feedback?	
Call Received: 09:28:46	04/08/2013

Incident Created	09:28:46
Address Validated	09:29:10
Incident confirmed	09:33:07
Transfer Sent	09:33:10
Resource Dispatched	10:29:07
Arrival At Scene	10:35:46
Resource Cleared	10:59:27
Incident Resulted	

CRIME NUMBER - @INC RELATION - CB/04469/13-9: REQUESTED BY OPERATOR 4447

Qualifiers:	
DISPOSAL QUALIFIERS	Domestic Abuse
DISPOSAL QUALIFIERS	Vulnerable CYP
ISR Comments	
CALLER REPORTING THAT NIKOLAS MARTINS IS BANGING ON HER DOOR	09:30:21
POLICE WERE LOOKING FOR HIM YESTERDAY	09:30:33
CALLER STATES HE IS NOT ALLOWED AT THE ADDRESS SHE STATES THERE ARE ISSUES AT THE ADDRESS AND HE IS NOT ALLOWED TO ATTEND	09:31:05
XXXXXXXX VULNERABLE MARKER MOP1 GROUP 2	09:33:04
MALE WAS RECENTLY ARRESTED FOR THEFT AND IMMIGRATION OFFENCES 28/07/2013	09:36:53
FURTHER CALL FROM NICOLETTE ASKING FOR OFFICERS AS EX STILL	09:38:42

OUTSIDE – ADVISED WE ARE AWARE AND WILL BE WITH HER ASAP	
CURRENTLY NMA	09:48:43
MALE IS NOT IN THE AREA	10:37:48
RESUMING FROM THIS INCIDENT	10:58:30
VP REPORT FOR CHILD TO BE SUBMITTED	10:59:16
THERE IS ALREADY AN OPEN DT WITH CAIU REFERRAL IN PLACE, WORKING SHEET HAS BEEN ADDED TO THAT REPORT AND CR ADDED TO THIS INCIDENT	13:26:19
Result Code: 'CUA', 'NR'	02:00:29
NO. of Arrests N.F.A No. of Reports	02:00:29
Handling Officer: 4447	02:00:29
Qualifiers, Vulnerable CYP, Domestic Abuse	02:00:29

On this day of the police incident report, he had been at the house for at least two hours on and off prior to me calling the police. I was afraid that if I did not call them one of the neighbours would and I would get into trouble. My little girl also begged me not to call the police. There had been too much police presence, and my children were afraid at the sight of them. In this instance, they managed to locate the police marker, but it took police over an hour to arrive at scene even though the marker was in place. For those three hours, I suffered abuse and terror. The police could not locate him, he was always one step ahead, and he was not done with me. He came back later that night to terrorise me yet again.

ISR Report

LEICESTERSHIRE POLICE

04/08/2013 23:47:31	PQA, CONCERN FOR SAFETY	LEP-040813-0895/LEP	999
Priority: (2) Priority	EX OUTSIDE	CB01	Officer Dealing: 7712
Operator: 7375	Dispatcher: 6479	CB01 (XXXXX,306032)	Creator Wkstn: BC21

ADDRESS INFORMATION:

XXX NEW PARKS BOULEVARD LEICESTER, LE3 9SA	Disposition code:
	DOMESTIC INC
Proximity:	
Complainant Information:	Theme:
NICOLETTE WALLACE	PUBLIC SAFETY
XXX NEW PARKS BOULEVARD LEICESTER LE3 9SA	
VICTIM [?] Media Consent [?] Feedback?	

Call Received: 23:47:31	04/08/2013

~ 168 ~

Incident Created	23:47:31
Address Validated	23:47:42
Incident confirmed	23:48:36
Transfer Sent	23:48:38
Resource Dispatched	23:52:39
Arrival At Scene	00:00:47
Resource Cleared	01:40:31
Incident Resulted	

CRIME NUMBER - @INC RELATION - CB/04497/13-5 : REQUESTED BY OPERATOR 7712

ISR Comments	
EX PARTNER OUTSIDE	23:48:48
WHISTLING	23:48:51
KNOCKING AND MAKING NOISE	23:49:00
HE IS WALKING AWAY	23:49:07
NIKOLAS MARTINS – 35YRS	23:49:26
NO ADDRESS FOR HIM	23:49:30
CALLED POLICE EARLIER – NO INC NUMBER KNOWN	23:49:40
POLICE COULD NOT LOCATE HIM	23:50:09
HE HAS NOW COME BACK AND IS OUTSIDE NOW – BLACK MALE WEARING BLACK LEATHER JACKET AND YELLOW T-SHIRT AND SOME JEANS APPEARS INTOXICATED	23:50:16
THIS KEEPS HAPPENING ANS SOCIAL SERVICES ARE INVOLVED. NO THREATS HE JUST TRYING TO GET IN	23:51:13
INC NUMBER GIVEN AND ADVISED WE WOULD ATTEND AS SOON AS ABLE.	23:54:19

REPEAT VICTIM, INFO BAR SHOWS PREVIOUS INCIDENTS, NHBP N/A, NOT DEEMED VULNERABLE, GENIE NOT DONE AS GRADE 2	
Result Code: 'PDC', 'NR'	02:04:02
NO. of Arrests N.F.A No. of Reports	02:04:02
Handling Officer: 7712	02:04:02
Qualifiers, Domestic Abuse	02:04:02

****

It Is What It Is

ISR Report

LEICESTERSHIRE POLICE

24/08/201 3 00:21:12	CHA, HARASSMEN T	LEP-240813- 0032/LEP	999
Priority: (2) Priority	BEING FOLLOWED BY EX	CB01	Officer Dealing : 7029
Operator: 5073	Dispatcher: 0872	CB01 (455644,XXXXX)	Creator Wkstn: BC25

ADDRESS INFORMATION:

XXX NEW PARKS BOULEVARD LEICESTER,	Disposition code:
	DOMESTIC INC
Proximity: FIRE STATION	
Complainant Information:	Theme:
NICOLETTE WALLACE	PUBLIC SAFETY
XXX NEW PARKS BOULEVARD LEICESTER LE3 9SA	
VICTIM [?] Media Consent [?] Feedback?	

Call Received: 00:21:11	24/08/2013

Incident Created	00:21:11
Address Validated	00:21:58
Incident confirmed	00:23:06
Transfer Sent	00:23:43
Resource Dispatched	01:34:52
Arrival At Scene	01:35:26
Resource Cleared	03:15:01
Incident Resulted	

CRIME NUMBER - @INC RELATION - CB/04469/13-9 : REQUESTED BY OPERATOR 7029

ISR Comments	
CALLER REPORTS THAT SHE IS BEING FOLLOWED BY EX PARTNER	00:23:29
CALLER IS WALKING HOME NOW	00:23:34
CALLER HAS HER TWO CHILDREN WITH HER — SHE HAS BEEN AT WEATHERSPOON'S AND MALE STARTED TO FOLLOW HER	00:24:05
CALLER STATES THE MALE IS DRUNK AND IS NOT MEANT TO BE CONTACTING HER OR HER CHILDREN	00:24:30
INFO BAR CHECKED NO RELEVANT INFO	00:26:04
REPEAT VICTIM BECAUSE REPORTED PREVIOUSLY	00:26:14
VULNERABILITY CONSIDERED, NOTHING TO SUGGEST THIS	00:26:19
NPB CHECKED N/A HISTORY CHECKED N/A	00:26:27

TRIED RINGING TO SEE IF CALLER GOT HOME OK- RINGS OUT TO V/M NO MESSAGE LEFT AS MAILBOX FULL	01:20:46
MALE HAS GONE ON HIS WAY	01:36:41
MALE MAY HAVE RETURNED TO ADDRESS	03:04:49
CHECKED AREA AND MALE NOT SEEN, FEMALE STATED SHE HAD NOT SEEN BIM BUT HEARD SOMEONE ON THE PATHWAY AND THOUGHT IT WAS HIM. SEARCHED AREA AND NOTHING SUGGESTED THIS	03:17:18
NO. of Arrests N.F.A No. of Reports	
Handling Officer:	
Qualifiers, None Apply	

I had taken the children out, and when returning home, we met with Nik, who began following us. I tried to make him leave us alone to no avail and then I had to call the police. I reported this incident to the social worker, and I was appalled by his report of events. He alleged that we had been spotted by a witness 'walking with' Nikolas— one of many examples that made me lose faith in the system. Situations like this arise when information is twisted, and a mother's credibility has no value.

This was the last ever incident I reported to the police personally. Any police involvement after that was as a result of someone else calling them, either a passer-by or neighbour. I was too exhausted mentally and I was close to a breakdown. I felt helpless with the situation at hand.

It had been three years of constant abuse, and my esteem had plummeted to rock bottom. I felt worthless as a person and worse as a mother. I had failed to protect my children by exposing them to violent situations which recurred around them.

CHAPTER 8

When I first met Nik, I was also broken, but he had managed to break me even more. I was no longer capable of making constructive decisions. My mind had been battered. I looked everywhere for a sign of help, but there was none to be found. I felt so empty and so alone. I feared for my life and the future of my children. Friends and family were disappointed in me. They were tired of my constant sob stories, so I shut them out. Social services were watching me like a hawk, waiting to pounce, while Nik on the other hand, was not backing down. The thought of taking my own life came to me but when I looked at my children, I could not go through with it. I was all they had, they needed me.

Nik was my abuser, but he also became the very same person I went to for comfort, often finding myself tangled in his web of deceit all over again. Each time he came back promising he would really make some changes and beg me to help him. He even showed me papers that proved he was getting help and that he was attending alcohol meetings. He said he was doing it all for me. Stupidly, I would believe him so that I could enjoy the man I first fell in love with.

One afternoon he stated that he missed the girls and me and wanted to see me. It was too risky for him to come over to the house, so we went to him instead. At that time he still lived in Upperton Road, Leicester. I prepared some food for him and packed it in a metal bowl and off we went. I suspected he was not eating because he could not afford to; he had lost so much weight. The little money he received from NASS he preferred to spend on alcohol and when he did not have money to buy that, he would rob the store. These were the rumours, although I never witnessed any of the occurrence, they were believable because he drank every day and was drunk every day. That does not happen on £35.00 a week - even if one's buying the cheapest drink. In his case, White Ace, which was £3.00 for three-litres with a volume of 7.5% alcohol. He used to call it *"take me quick"*.

On that day we were both drinking whilst the children watched TV and played games. The day went by and everything was fine, and everybody was getting along. During the night I felt hungry and I remembered the food I had brought for Nik. I got up and went to the kitchen. I did not bother to put some on a plate or to heat it. I just carried the bowl as it was back to the bedroom then sat next to where he lay dozing off. I heard him move and then all of a sudden like a flash of lighting, he struck me on the mouth with the metal bowl.

"That's my food!" he bellowed at me as he sat up, staring at me. Then I saw blood pouring out of my mouth and the food scattered all over the place. My mouth hurt, and there was a funny feeling inside it, so I ran my tongue around my mouth. I was shocked and horrified; I had no front tooth! He broke my front tooth! I became hysterical. I screamed and yelled in agony. I was also in physical pain but mostly it was my heart that took most of the beating. What had I done to deserve it? He just sat there watching me as the blood poured out of my mouth, and I sobbed. The girls looked on in a terrified state.

I immediately phoned his mother because she was the only person I could speak to about the abuse her son was dishing out to me. It was around three o'clock in the morning. I was still crying, and I told her what had happened. She told me she had just finished a double shift and would call me as soon as she woke up. When Nik's roommate saw the bad situation, he offered to drive the children and me back home. Nik was indifferent. I got nothing from him. He seemed confused and detached. I did not speak to him; I could not even look at him. When we arrived home, I put the girls to sleep and went to the bathroom to look in the mirror.

"Oh my God!" I cried until I could not cry any more. I was missing a front tooth. Nik had knocked out my front tooth; over what? Food? My food? I had no explanation for his behaviour. I was normally good at making excuses for him, but this time I was shooting blanks. I went downstairs to the kitchen, opened a bottle of wine and began to drink. Because of social services, I was not allowed contact with Nik, which meant I was not supposed to have been at his flat on that day. How was I going to explain such an injury to people, Angel's school bus staff, Star's teachers, parents, friends_, anybody? I could not wear a wig that covered my mouth like I had hidden all the other injuries. I used my mouth to talk and to speak, I had to open my mouth. There was no way around it. My lip was a bit swollen but most of the damage was inside where the soft flesh had made contact with my tooth.

I often heard stories that if you saw a woman with a missing tooth in the front it meant she was a prostitute because they got beat up by their pimps or by one of their many clients. When I looked in the mirror at that moment, that is what I saw: a cheap whore. I ached. I never went to sleep that night. I continued drinking and crying feeling hopeless and helpless. I was injured and yet I had no one to talk to. I had been violated, yet I could not reach out to the police or anyone else in authority. Instead, I plotted lies to cover up my own iniquities. I was also building a web of lies to cover up for my tormenter. The abuse continued because of this.

He now had full authority over me. There was no one else out there for me. He had managed to isolate me from the rest of the world. I had not seen or spoken to Nina and Minty in a while. I was not communicating with my family and apart from our circle of friends, (which was also problematic), I had nobody else. I made an emergency appointment with the dentist who fortunately gave me an appointment for first thing that Monday morning. That day

I devised a trick to cover my mouth with a scarf claiming I had a toothache; if anyone asked. It worked. I told my dentist that I slipped in the bathtub and hit my tooth against the tap. He did not believe me, but I was not there to be believed, I was there to protect my family.

"Next time you have a problem talk to your own mother. Don't phone my mum she's not your mother!" Was the text sent to me by Nik after knocking out my tooth. I do not know what they talked about because she never called me back and I did not pursue it. I told her what her son had done to me so at least I knew she was aware of the monster she had borne. This was not the first incident I had shared with his mother. There were more before that and plenty after. Even when he stole from me and emptied my bank account, I relayed it all to her.

My phone did not stop ringing or beeping, and by the time I woke up one morning, there was a total of 218 missed calls. I thought I was going insane, and the phones were not stopping.

"Do you want to see me in a psychiatric hospital? Is that what you want? Are you deliberately trying to push me to the edge so that I get sectioned and lose everything? Why are you doing this? WHY?" I screamed down the line and hung up, but that did not stop him. He came to the house later that day waking the whole neighbourhood declaring his love for me and at the same time calling me a bitch because I would not acknowledge him. In his mind, I did not appreciate his efforts to show me love.

The next morning there was a knock at my door. I went to answer it and saw my neighbour standing there.

"Did you know your car was broken into last night?"

"What?"

We walked to my car and there was shattered glass everywhere. The window to the driver's side was smashed but nothing was taken. My car was broken. I was broken. I knew who had done it. It did not take a genius to work it out. I was mortified. How could someone say they loved me and yet cause so much distress and destruction? He knew it cost money to repair the window, he knew my children depended on the car as their main mode of transport. My neighbour helped me board it up and then Nik appeared from nowhere.

I reported my car to the police, but they said they could not carry the case further as there were no witnesses even though I told them who had done it. I took pictures of the damage and took them to the social worker. I pointed out how serious and dangerous the situation was getting and requested to be moved from the address. I told him that I was ready to make a new start elsewhere as long as it was as far away from Nikolas Martins as possible. I had started looking on the web for a potential house swap and also had started looking for special schools that accommodated children with autism. It was a dark period for me.

The social worker argued that Angel was settled in her current school and that any changes would affect her but what he failed to acknowledge was that she was already being affected by what was going on at home. First, there was a broken dining-room window, then a broken bedroom window (which I had shown to his mum when she visited), now the car - not to mention all that blood spilling in front of the children. I asked social services repeatedly, to assist us in moving to a different town, but I got no help from anyone.

I could not make the move on my own without school reports or reports and recommendations from the local authority, so I was stuck. For me to move from one special school to the other I would need the local authority to assist in housing, but I was barking up the wrong tree. I tried to do it myself, but it was hopeless. I kept hitting dead ends. It was frustrating and strenuous. I was all alone and very afraid. I feared for my children, and I feared for their future. I was in a catch-22 situation; a battle I could not win no matter which ally I chose. I was fighting a losing battle and it was the most terrifying feeling ever. A feeling of hopelessness and feeling open to attack, being a victim and being vulnerable made me easy prey to my tormenter and he knew it.

One time, he followed me home and assaulted me the whole way, slapping me and punching me because I would not acknowledge him. I did not have the children on that day. My brother was looking after them at home. Nik was demanding to know where the girls were and where I had been. After a while, a police car pulled up in front of us and two police officers came out.

"We have received a call from a member of the public reporting that there was a male attacking a female fitting your description", the female officer said.

I denied the allegations because I knew what would happen. If they found it to be true, they would have to conduct investigations and - would find out about social services' involvement, -so they would have an obligation to notify them of the incident. I was not about to let that happen. We both gave false names and denied any assault. However, they did not believe us and arrested Nik anyway. I never told my brother what had happened. I just suffered in silence and sought solace in alcohol.

Another, time Nik came to the house, and we had an altercation. As he was throwing punches, I took a glass from the table and threw it at him, but it missed and smashed on the wall. Then during the fight, he pushed me on to the ground, where I fell on some broken glass that left a deep wound on my left buttock. I actually had to pull the glass out because it was embedded in me. There was blood everywhere, and I bled for hours. I never called the police nor did I seek medical attention. I did not want to answer the relevant questions, so I let it go and treated my wounds with more alcohol. To this date, I have a big scar on my left buttock_, another reminder of the savagery I endured.

Over a period of years, things had been going missing around the house. It was frustrating and driving me crazy because I could never establish where things were disappearing to or who was taking stuff from my house. Nik and I would sit down and try to come up with a suspect amongst our friends, but It was always hard for me to come up with a name. I trusted them. One morning Star was missing her DS game.

"Have you seen Star's pink Nintendo game?" I asked him one morning after I had searched everywhere.

"No sorry sweetheart, I will help you look."

I could not bear to watch my child go without her favourite game. She spent most of her free time on the gadget. She seemed lost without it and it broke my heart. I looked again in the places I had looked before, still no joy.

"Star are you sure you didn't take it to school by accident?" I asked. It was a long shot because I knew she would never take her game to school; she knew better. Next day after dropping her off to school I went to the bank and withdrew some money from our savings and replaced the game. She was over the moon when she came back home to her new toy. Seeing the joy on her face was priceless. I never gave up looking for her old game, each time I cleaned the house, I would look for it. It had to be in the house somewhere.

More things started to go missing from the house-:, the children's games consoles, my camcorder (with memories and all), phones, cameras, even my leather jacket which was hung in the hallway along with other coats. I started to suspect Mika and Seth. They were good people and had been very protective of my family, but because they were both alcoholic. I thought they might have been stealing to feed their habit. I had other people come in and out of my house, although not as often as before, but the circle was very limited to Leo, Marcy, Kimberley, Thomas, Marnie and Nina. It was a mystery for a long time until one day I had a mini barbeque.

We were listening to music and watching the children play. We ran out of coal and I asked Nik to rush to the shops to get more. As usual, he did not refuse; the word 'no' did not exist in his dictionary. As he reached out for his coat, something fell from the pocket. I looked down and got the shock of my life-: it was Angel's Nintendo game. Unlike Star, Angel could not communicate that she could not find her game, and she usually played on it in her room, so I did not notice that it was missing. My whole body was overcome with rage. I ran to the kitchen, took a steak knife, and headed towards him before one of the guests stopped me.

"I will kill you! How could you? How could you steal from your own family? Stealing from your daughters, the daughters you claim to love and care about!" I went on ranting and raving with the guy still restraining me whilst another took the knife carefully from my hands.

"Get the fuck outta here and don't ever come back! You are evil! All this time we've been missing things from the house, it was YOU!" I was angry and hurt.

Some of our guests advised him to leave because they saw how enraged I was and were trying to stop the situation from escalating. He left and I burst into tears. I was devastated. I was looking after him in every way. I fed him, gave him a place to sleep and even fed his dirty habit and yet he was stealing from us. Stealing from my children! I was hurt and humiliated in front of acquaintances. It was a very sad situation indeed.

In total, he stole over £2000,00 from me, either by stealing my bank cards and clearing cash out, or going through my pockets, searching for money. As for the gadgets he stole, they amount to over £3000.00. He targeted mostly my children's toys because he knew I could not see my girls go without and he knew I would easily replace those. This took place for over four years and despite the ugliness I saw, I still hoped for a miracle. I was in too deep; I could not see the light. I was grieving the loss of his old self. He physically attacked me in public places, in friends' houses, in my own home and yet I did nothing. I was mentally paralysed.

Although this was all going on, there was not a single day that the social worker came to my house to find me drunk or drinking. My children were well cared for, had 100% attendance at school and were always well presented. All school records showed developing and progressing children in every aspect. I had unannounced visits for over four years. Even though they found no fault in my household or the girls' welfare, they pressed me on the matter of Nik. Each statement I made was twisted to make me look bad. Nothing I said was ever recorded as it was. I felt under attack.

I will forever live with the decisions I made at that time, despite my mental state. I was willing to go against my good nature and good sense to get his love and undivided attention. I thought because he loved me, he would heal the wounds from my past. I thought he was the one I had been waiting for to finally make all the pain and suffering go away. But he ended up being the one that brought me to total destruction. It was the love I had for my children that kept me hanging on.

~ ~ ~

On the 9th of February 2014, I was awakened by loud banging on my front door. I looked at the clock and it was just before six o'clock in the morning, then there was more banging.

"Sweetheart open the door!" then I heard thumping and kicking. "Open the door bitch I want to take a shit!" he shouted flapping the mailbox loudly and banging on the window. It was a Sunday morning and the whole neighbourhood was quiet and still asleep.

"If you don't open this door now, I'm going to take a shit right here on your doorstep!" He kept shouting obscenities. The children were asleep, and I did not want them to be awakened by the racket, so I jumped out of bed and rushed downstairs. I did not open the door because I already knew the state he was in; drowned in alcohol. I spoke to him through the window.

"Nik why are you doing this? You know the trouble I have with social services, but you still come here at odd hours making trouble. Do you want me to lose my children? Do you?! Is that what you want, Nik?"

"Sorry sweetheart, it's just that you were not opening the door, please let me in", he said slurring his words but much calmer.

"Not in that state I will not, besides, after all the attention you have attracted, one of the neighbours might have phoned the police already and if they come and find you here, you know what will happen. I am sorry I ain't risking my children for you, not any more Nik." I moved away from the window and went back upstairs, checked on the girls who were both still fast asleep.

In all the time I had known him and been with him or seen him, I would honestly say, on that particular day; Nik was at rock bottom. He was using language he had never used before and appeared completely incognisant of his surroundings. So wasted, empty and alone. Six o'clock in the morning and he was wandering on the street. I had never seen such a troubled soul; my heart went out to him. I wanted to reach out to him and help him, but my hands were tied. I was only a week away from social services removing my children from the child protection register because they were convinced that we had not had any contact with Nik. I was not about to risk that. As much as I loved him, I had a lot more to lose.

From my bedroom window, I watched as he paced up and down the front garden. I watched him drink some more and his co-ordination was limited. At one point, he stumbled and fell over. Suddenly, after a few more minutes of banging, it went quiet. I thought he might have fallen asleep at the doorstep, so I looked down from my bedroom window, which was directly above the front door, I could not see him. Then, he emerged from around the garden, and I immediately popped my head back in to avoid any more drama. He tried knocking some more, but I ignored him. At that point, I was so scared that one of the neighbours might phone the police and if that happened, I would be in trouble for not contacting them first. I was required to report each time he turned up at the address.

Failure to do so would lead to social services being involved.

Moments later, I watched him as he staggered towards the gate, which he bumped into. He was carrying three plastic bags containing tinned foods and some other food bits, so I knew he had been to the food bank at some point during the week. But then this was Sunday morning and he was still walking around with the bags, a clear indication that he was indeed homeless. I knew he was in serious trouble. It was so sad to watch. I felt so helpless. He struggled to walk and was tussling with his trousers which kept falling because he had lost so much weight. He looked ghastly. I had never cried for Nik the way I cried for him on that day. I watched him walk away until he faded away into the long boulevard. As I watched him, I cried and prayed; I never took my eyes off him the whole time. My heart was breaking for him. I will never forget that image for as long as I live. I wanted to help him, but we had become worlds apart. *"What happened to my Nikolas?"* Once he faded into the distance. I knelt down beside my bed and prayed, tears rolling down my cheeks.

"Dear God, how much more does a man have to suffer
before you rescue him?
Six o'clock on a Sunday morning he is wandering the
streets,
drunk to oblivion and headed in no direction.
Why can you not put a rest to this man and let his soul
rest in peace?

All the doors have been shut for him from both friends and family.
*I tried talking to his mother, asking her to come and save him, but even **she;** could not help him.*
I went to the lengths of communicating with his dead father,
for him to look after his son because his soul is calling out for help, and I cannot help him.
Lord, you know my hands are tied, I wish I could save him, but it has gone beyond me.
I love him, and I think he should be in a better place. No human being deserves to live like that.
And please Lord, I do not want to lose my children; each time he turns up here in that state,
I am compromised and I cannot deal with it any longer, I need you Lord, now more than ever.
This situation has become too big for me to deal with, I am helpless.
By rescuing Nik, you will be saving me, so, please, Father, help me. Come quickly to save me".
AMEN"

It was a desperate prayer from a desperate and broken woman.

My aunt Marjorie still lived in Peterborough an hour's drive away and I had not seen her in years. I was the closest relative to her geographically, yet I was the only one who had never been to her house. I decided to put the past behind us and contacted her. I was also trying to rebuild my life without Nik, and I needed a distraction, so I thought of the idea of taking regular trips to her and spend afternoons or weekends with her.

Two weeks before Valentine's Day in 2014 we arranged to visit her the following weekend and have lunch with her. It was all set; I had done some shopping to take with us and I also prepared some food to contribute to her feast since she said she had invited some of her friends. I made a fruit salad, vegetable salad, samosas, and spring rolls. I bought a few snacks and two bottles of red wine. I told the girls of the plans and we were all excited about the trip. I was also trying to get away from Nik by detaching myself slowly. I thought that if he came to the house when we were not in, that would deter him, and he would give up.

On the morning of 15th February, after breakfast, I bathed my girls and got them ready for our much-anticipated journey to Peterborough. I got myself ready and we all went into the car to buy some more bits and pieces for our lunch, then took the car for servicing and a wash. We went back home, and I started loading everything into the car. Just as I was about to switch off switches and lock up, my house phone rang.

"Hi Nico, I am so sorry I know we arranged this trip a while ago, but I am afraid we will have to cancel it. I went out to the club last night and only came home a couple of hours ago and I am really tired. Can we do this tomorrow?"

That was my aunt on the other end of the phone. I could not believe it, a few more seconds and we would have been on the road. The girls were ready and looking forward to it. It would affect Angel the most because it took time to prepare her for the journey. She was aware that on that day we were going to see Auntie Marj in Peterborough.

"Why didn't you call me last night or first thing in the morning? We were just about to get into the car?"

"I thought I could do it, but I am too tired to even stay awake. I have also told my friends not to come today. Why don't you come tomorrow, we will do it tomorrow instead, yes."

I was extremely disappointed because we had arranged this trip two weeks prior. I went to the car and put everything back in the fridge. I had to explain to the children that there was no more going to Peterborough. It took Angel a long time to settle because she kept repeating, *"Peterborough, Auntie Marjorie"*. I was devastated for her; she did not understand. I took them into town for shopping instead, and then we went to Nando's for a special treat.

When we got back home, we played in the garden for a while then I put the karaoke CD on, and we enjoyed singing and dancing until bedtime. I tucked them in, read their bedtime stories and made my way downstairs for some much needed 'me' time. I became lonely and I was still upset with my aunt. I put on a film and went into the kitchen to open a bottle of wine which I had purchased for our trip to Peterborough and began to drink. I felt the emptiness in my life. I did not understand the feeling because I had two gorgeous girls sleeping upstairs who meant the world to me. Yet I still felt very alone. Although Angel was now eleven years old, she still had not developed her communication. She spoke only using words and never responded to anything. Instead, she would repeat back to me everything I said to her. I could not reach out to her; she was in a completely different world of her own. It broke my heart each and every day.

"Oh God, why can't you make her speak_? She can still be autistic but please just make her talk to me and understand me. The barrier between us is unbearable. She is with me but not really with me. Please make her talk, that is all I ask, for you to give my baby girl the ability to speak. Right now, she cannot understand, why we did not travel to Peterborough. I couldn't make her understand and she couldn't make me understand her feelings. It is heart-breaking Father. Please Lord; Please I beg you, make her talk to me_." I prayed inside as tears rolled down my cheeks. I finished the first bottle of wine and opened the other.

I thought of Nik and how distressing it was for me to watch him waste away. I thought about where he could be and what he was doing. Whether he had eaten or found somewhere to sleep for the night and all the other past nights. My heart bled for him. I was in love with the guy and yet we could not be together. I also did not understand how I could still be in love with a man that treated me so brutally. The man who controlled my life, beat me, and stole from me. But then I thought of Mike, Cuba, and Roderick; it was a pattern. A vicious cycle, one that I found hard to escape from. I really missed Nik and wished things had been different. Social services had threatened to take my children away from me if I kept seeing him.

Just as I was about to get up and go to the kitchen to pour myself a glass of wine, there was a knock at the door. I looked at the time and it was just after midnight. I went and opened the door. It was Nik. I just found myself running into his arms, and he held me so tight like he would not let go. Without thinking of the consequences, I let him in. He was holding a bag which contained a three-litre bottle of Ace cider. He noticed that I had been crying and I explained to him why. I talked about the failed trip to Peterborough and Angel's condition, but I neglected to tell him that I was just thinking of him seconds before he knocked on my door.

He followed me into the kitchen where he helped himself to a glass and poured himself a drink and I did the same. Then we sat down on the floor in the lounge. We talked about anything and everything that night. I told him that I was risking my children's lives by letting him in the house and at the same time I could not turn him away because of the deep love I felt for him. Especially after I had seen him six days earlier in the state he was. I wanted to hold him and wish for everything to be all right; no alcohol and no violence just us enjoying a family life together. I knew it was too late for that, but I so desperately wished for it.

To speak honestly, I had reached the end of my tether. On the one hand, I had social services threatening to take my children if I opened the door for Nik. On the other hand, I had Nik threatening violence if I did not open the door which would involve the police and the police had a duty to notify social services because there were children involved. I was in a no-win situation; I was headed for disaster and only God could help me. I was being pulled from both sides; I had lost control of my life yet again. I was also failing my children.

That night was an amazing one. We shared our deepest feelings and fears. He talked about how much it affected him, knowing that his son Ted was being brought up by another man and that he could not even provide for him financially. He talked about how he missed his dad and how he thought he would never get over his death. His father had died at a significant time as well, ten days before Christmas. He always remembered and talked about him even though he had died when Nik was only thirteen years old; he was now thirty-six. He talked about his love for me, and said that he had never felt the way he did for me with any woman before.

We looked at each other deeply, as if our souls were communicating. He took my hand and led me up the stairs into my bedroom. We had never made love like we did on this night. We did everything you can possibly think of that two people in love do. They say love is sweet when you share it with the one you love; and that person loves you back. That night was proof that in his own wicked way, he absolutely loved me. The feeling was beautiful, more than words can express. It was right then and there, that I knew, disaster was inevitable. I was on board yet again, on another hazardous train; on the rails to disaster.

He looked straight into my eyes as he thrust himself inside me. "Ahhh! I love you, Nikolas Martins!" I cried out. I was in tears as he made sweet love to me. It was passionate and very emotional. I wanted him and yet I could not have him. The birds began to sing, as if they were singing for us; it was dawn and he was still making love to me. It was a special and gratifying night; definitely a night to remember. We only got out of bed to prepare the children's breakfast. We had no plans for the day, so we had decided to spend it together, but we could not risk being seen together. He made breakfast whilst I drove to the shops and bought another bottle of wine and a bottle of Ace Cider. We intended to chill, take it easy and stay indoors that Sunday. He wanted to make up for missing Valentine's Day with me, so we decided to celebrate our Valentine's on the 16th of February 2014. "Happy Valentines!" we said to each other, clicking our glasses.

My land line kept ringing but I chose to ignore it. Star was watching Nickelodeon on the TV downstairs and Angel was on her computer in her bedroom. Both my mobile phone and landline were ringing like crazy, but I decided to ignore the calls. I had everyone I needed with me under the same roof. Eventually, I decided to look at the phones to see who had been calling. When I checked both phones there were seventeen missed calls on my cell phone and six frantic messages from my Aunt Marjorie. I listened to the voice messages and she sounded frenzied in all of them. Nik and I were cuddled up in bed loving each other and drinking. As I was scrolling through my mobile phone a call came in reflecting her number.

"Hello?"

"I have been trying to reach you all morning. What time are you leaving the house because I know it takes you an hour to get here?" That was my Aunt Marjorie on the other end of the phone. I told her that I was no longer planning to travel to her house.

"No, no, no you can't do this to me, I have been preparing lunch all morning and I made loads of food and invited my friends over. They want to meet you and the children so you cannot let me down. Get yourselves ready and start making your way."

"Okay," I replied. I figured if I just agreed with her, she would settle down because she was in a real panic. As soon as I put the phone down, I cuddled up with Nik, not planning on going anywhere.

A couple of hours later the phones were ringing again. "Where are you?" I heard my aunt screaming from the other end. "All my friends are here, waiting for you. We planned this meet-up two weeks ago and we spoke about it yesterday." I could not believe the cheek. She had cancelled on us at the last minute and now she was putting pressure on me!

"We are on our way, don't worry_," I responded. I was not in the mood, but then suddenly, I thought, instead of spending the whole day hiding ourselves in the house it would be nice to have a change of scenario out of Leicester where nobody knew us.

"It will give me a chance to talk to your aunt. I want to tell her how I feel about you, maybe she can understand me. I want to tell her that I want you to be my wife," said Nik. "Trust me, my aunt does not like you one little bit, she is aware of all the trouble you have caused, I tell her everything. She knows each and every scar you left on my body and she is also aware that I invited your mum over."

"That is why I want to meet her and tell her my side of the story."

"Yeah, and what side is that, that you can justify hurting me?

"Nico, please let me talk to her, "he pleaded.

I looked at the clock, and it had gone just after one pm. I called the girls, got them ready and explained to them that we were going to Peterborough after all. I loaded all the food into the car, locked up and headed out. Straight away I noticed something unusual. All the times we had travelled in the car, Angel always sat on the passenger's seat because she liked controlling the music on the main CD player. It was well- known to my friends and family, so anyone who caught a ride with us would sit with Star at the back because the front seat was always reserved for our DJ Angel.

"Star did you tell Angel to sit in the back?" I asked as I noticed Angel sitting next to her in the back seat all strapped up.

"No Mum she just opened the door and came in by herself."

"Are you sure?" I asked again because it had never happened before, it was out of character. Even Nik commented on it as he opened the passenger's door. Angel was wearing her headphones and listening and watching music on the other DVD player. Star did not switch hers on as she preferred to colour in instead. Although it was extremely unusual and significant, I let it pass. But I remained baffled.

"Oh no, you are not coming into the car with that_," I said to Nik, who was holding his three-litre bottle of cider, half of which he had finished. I did not want any alcohol in the car in case we got stopped by the police. We were already breaking the rules by being together, so I did not want extra trouble. He got out of the car and instead of throwing it away he gulped it down his throat. In under a minute, he had consumed about one-and-a-half litres of cider!

"Wow!" I managed to say, as he came and took a seat beside me. We were on our journey to Peterborough.

"I love you, Nicolette_; you are my wife, till death do us part. I am never going to leave you because I have fallen deeply in love with you. God gave you to me, you just don't know it yet and I am going to explain all this to your aunt."

"You mean you are obsessed with me_," I laughed as I joked with him.

"I love you Nic, and today I am going to declare my love for you to your family," he said. By this time, the alcohol had entered his system. He looked wasted. I did not want him to meet my aunt in that state, and I told him so. We argued a bit about it. I told him that I was going to stop the car and let him out. He was too drunk to be amongst other people. I did not wish to be humiliated. I drove on and as we were about to join the A47 motorway just outside Leicester, he asked me to stop the car because he wanted to take a leak. I did so; and as soon as he was out of sight, I drove off.
"Mum, what are you doing? You can't just leave him here!" I heard Star speak. I stopped the car just after a few yards and looked back to see him emerging from the hidden bushes. I reversed the car.

"Were you just going to leave me out here?" he asked with a serious face. I tried to avoid confrontation, so I laughed it off.

"I was just teasing," I said, but he did not look impressed. We got into the A47, and we were on our way to Aunt Marjorie in Peterborough. We talked and laughed and were listening to music, having a blast. The road was nice and quiet, it being a Sunday afternoon. I looked at the time, and it was coming up to two forty-five pm. We continued to talk and laugh; Angel was busy with her music DVD and Star was colouring in. All was good. When the Gyptian song, 'Nah Let Go' started playing. Nik began singing along and instead of '*she* nah let go', he sang, '*me* nah let go'. He kept playing Sean Paul's 'Like Glue', singing to me, "*I don't really care what people say: I don't really watch what dem waan do_ Still I got to stick to my girl like glue; and I mon nah play number two*" This song was sung to me a million times over the years, all Sean Paul's tunes were. Nik was a true fan.

*"I said I want you I want you; I want you I want you_, I'll give you some time, even a little **while**.* I am never gonna let you go Nicolette; you are my wife forever. God gave you to me, till death do us part" he said, with a big grin on his face.

"Yeah, right." I brushed him off. It hurt me because I honestly believed that he genuinely loved me. But the demon; alcohol, had snatched him from the real world. Each time he said those words to me, my heart melted. I wanted them to be true. I wanted so desperately for us to be a normal couple and a proper family. Not only was it too late, but it had also proved impossible. I think the devil had snatched him long before he came into my life.

Oh, I so wanted us to love each other and care for one another. I was hoping my aunt could talk to him and make him see sense. I was hoping she could fix us; it was my last hope. Inviting his mother did not work, he carried on being the same person he had always been, so my aunt was the end of the road.

We were a few minutes away from the exit of A47 when suddenly, I lost control of the car. I was not sure what happened, it was as if I had been taken away for a few seconds. Even today, I try to make my mind take me back to that moment, but all it shows is a blank. I do not know what happened, because I was not there. All I heard was a loud and frantic voice; it was Nik shouting what were to be his last words.

"Babe, watch out!"

CRASH!

CHAPTER 9

Everything went quiet. The only sound I heard was Angel's humming. The smell of the air bags filled the car. I was in shock and confusion. The car had veered off the road and was now facing east where we had crashed into a wooden fence. Nik was slumped on his right above my left shoulder, blood pouring from his head onto my shoulder and dripping down my arm and dress. I looked back at the children and they were both covered in blood on their faces and clothes.

"Are you all right?" I asked, perplexed.

"Yeah," Star managed to answer. Angel's humming continued.

"Angel, are you okay?" I asked.

"Angel okay" she answered and continued humming.

"Babe c'mon we need to get out," I said to Nik shaking him gently, but he still remained slumped. His head almost touching my shoulder, blood pouring out. My left arm was all red, and the strong smell of his blood was overwhelming in my nose, almost choking as it travelled down my throat.

"Sweetheart! Nik! Nik wake up!" I screamed, trying to wake him, but he remained motionless.

"Nik c'mon we have to get out of the car." I said continuing to shake him gently, but still remained slouched and was not responding. I then noticed something sticking out from his head and then I looked at the windscreen and noticed a big hole in it. I assumed that the glass must have broken and was embedded in his head, so I reached out. The texture of the material did not feel like glass at all-: that is when I realised that I was not feeling glass, but the bone of his skull! My heart was pounding, I was in terror. Blood was pouring on me like water from a tap, fast and heavy, the smell so distinctive.

Just then I heard voices and saw people opening my door and the back doors of the car. I could hear voices but could not comprehend.

"Nik c'mon we have to get out of the car now" I shook him some more and there was no response. One man took my hand and helped me out of the car whilst another helped my children out. Everything was going in slow motion.

"Are you okay" I asked as I held both girls tight in my arms, still disorientated. I remember trying to go around to the passenger's seat to reach out to Nik, but someone blocked my way and turned me around leading me away from the wreckage. I was told that the ambulance was on its way and so were the police. I could feel my heart heavy in my chest. I felt as though I was dying just from the horror. I was wearing a yellow dress which was now half-red from Nik's blood. I could almost taste the strong smell of blood. I saw people gathering at the scene of the accident. There was a lot of movement and chaos. I could not make out what was taking place. Suddenly a police car arrived, followed by an ambulance. We were given a blanket each and led to safety. I was still in shock.

The medics were trying to get Nik out of the car, then after what seemed like ages, I heard the sound of a helicopter. It was the air ambulance. My mind was in a daze, not knowing which direction to go, I was lost. After a while, a police officer came to ask me some questions, I was shaking and asked to fetch my cigarettes from the car, but I was not allowed. Paramedics were still at the scene of the accident. I asked to go and see Nik, but I was not allowed that either. I gave the police officer details of my Aunt Marjorie so that he could notify her of the events. I was startled at the horrific scene a few metres away from me and kept replaying the crash in my mind.

"Babe, watch out!" Nik's voice kept echoing in my head. After what seemed to be an age, another police car pulled up, and I saw my Aunt seated in the passenger's seat.

"It's all your fault! You caused this!" I cried out, pointing my finger at her. She remained quietly seated in the police car. I did not know why I said that to her, it just came out the moment I saw her. I spoke without thinking. The children were placed in the same car and taken to Peterborough hospital. I guess because they had no physical injuries, they were not put in an ambulance. When they left, a police officer came to me and asked me to take a breathalyser test. I blew twice over the limit.

"Nicolette Wallace I am arresting you"_____.

I was still in a trance and did not hear the rest of his statement. I did not utter a word. The accident scene was now clear, and all that remained was my blue BMW, all cut up, and in the middle of nowhere. We were heading to the police station for a formal arrest. I was given a change of clothes when we arrived at the police station. They arrested me and gave me another alcohol test which again gave out a positive reading over twice the limit. My fingerprints and photographs were taken, and I was given bail until the 6th of May 2014. Two officers then drove me to Peterborough Hospital where Nik and the children had been admitted.

When I saw the girls, they had been cleaned up and also given a change of clothes. None of them had been hurt. Star had a little mark a few millimetres long on the side of her head and Angel had little spots on her right hand caused by the broken glass I had a small cut on my knee also caused by the flying glass. None of us had sustained any real injuries at all, but I heard that Nik was in a critical condition. I asked to see him, and I was told to wait because they were still working on him. My Aunt Marj was still with the children when I arrived at the hospital and I asked her to stay a bit longer so that she could see to the girls whilst I went to see Nik. The more they delayed, the more I worried. So, I approached one of the doctors on duty to ask about Nik's condition.

"He suffered severe brain injuries and is in a critical condition. If he survives, it will be a miracle", were the doctor's exact words. I felt sick to my stomach. I did not know how I crashed the car and how Nik sustained such critical injuries. I could not really make out whether things were actually happening or whether I was having a nightmare. Nothing around me made any sense, a few hours prior, Nik and I were in bed making love. How had we ended up where we were?

After a long wait, with me pacing up and down, trying to come back to reality, the doctor came to fetch me and took me to Nik. He lay there, lifeless, with bandages all over his body and head. He had a tube in his mouth that connected him to the oxygen tank. The life-support machine is what was keeping him alive. All the years I had known him, I had never seen Nik so helpless and vulnerable. I could not stop the tears springing to my eyes. I sat next to his bed and held his hand as reality began sinking in. It was not a nightmare; I was actually living the moment. His injuries were horrific and again the stench of blood overtook me. I sat next to him and held his hand. He was nice and warm.

"Oh, Nik I'm so sorry. Please wake up and talk to me. Everything's gonna be all right, I am right here with you. You will pull through; we will pull through together. I am going to look after you. Doctor said your brain has taken a big hit, but it's okay, I'll take care of you for as long as it takes. We are going to be a proper family, you'll see. We will make it work; this is a sign. We *will* make it sweetheart"

"You know, he can't hear a word you are saying. His brain is gone. The piece of wood shattered his skull and smashed his brain," one of the Doctors said to me.

"No Doctor, if he hears my voice, he will wake up, you'll see," I responded as I looked back at Nik with so much hope inside me. "Look Doctor, his chest is going up and down which means he is breathing and therefore can hear me."

"It's the life support machine that is doing the breathing for him. We will be transferring him to Addenbrookes Hospital in a few minutes, so we will give you a few moments of privacy-." They walked out.

"I don't really care what people say:

I don't really watch what dem waan do.

Still I got to stick to my girl like glue; and I mon nah play number two" by Sean Paul.

"I said I want you I want you; I want you I want you.

*I'll give you some time, even a little **while...**"* by Gyptian.

I sang all his favourite songs to him. I sang and sang and cried and sang. If he did not respond to one song, I would sing another. His eyes were open, but they were not moving or blinking. I continued to sing as I desperately held on to his hand. I was trying to be strong for him, but I could not stop the tears. My sweetheart was not responding to me. He always responded to me. It was not looking good, but at that particular moment, I was not afraid, I believed deep down that if he heard my voice he would come back. After a few minutes, the doctors came back into the room. I continued singing and they looked at me with empathy on their faces.

"I'm afraid his transport is here, he has to be taken to a specialist hospital immediately," the doctor informed me. I really wished I could ride with him, but Aunt Marj had to go back to her house, and I could not leave my children alone in the hospital. As the doctors approached the bed, one of them shut Nik's eyes with his hand and started preparing him for the journey.

"I love you, sweetheart. Hang in there. I have to stay here with the girls, but I will come and be with you soon. I love you so much-." I gave him a long kiss goodbye, then I watched them wheel him away as our hands separated. I burst into tears, it felt like an illusion.

We were allocated three beds. Angel slept in one and Star and I shared the other. I held her tight all night long. It was a long night. I could not shut my eyes, I kept seeing Nik slumped in the car and blood pouring on me and then the image of him on the hospital bed with bandages all over and a tube in his mouth. I could not recall how the car left the road to hit a fence, that memory was blurred. All I remembered and still heard so clearly in my head, was Nik shouting, "Babe watch out!" and I could still smell the stench of his blood.

I thought of Nik's mom, I had to inform her, but I did not have my phone with me. I knew that the sight of Nik would definitely break her heart. Nevertheless, I had to reach out to her somehow. First thing the following morning, I asked at the reception to ring Addenbrookes Hospital to find out how Nik was doing. I spoke to one of the doctors in the neurological disease ward. He informed me that the situation was still critical, and that Nik was still on life support.

"Doctor, I don't know how you can help me reach his family. I don't have my phone with me, and it is important that I speak to his family and let them know what's happened."

"They have been notified, and they are already here," he replied.

"They are? Who is there with him?" I asked.

"His mother and brother."

"May I speak to his mother please?" I begged, and a few moments later I heard Mummy's voice.

"Mummy I am so sorry, please forgive me. I am really sorry. Are there any changes in his condition?" I said, as my whole body shivered.

"He's gone_" then there was silence. "My baby is gone," she cried. I was shaking and the words were echoing in my head. I was getting more confused by the unfolding events. I mean how could he be gone, I was talking to him just a few hours ago_? I was making sweet love to him several hours before, and I had three marks on my neck from his love bites to prove it. She cried and I cried, and we put the phones down.

Nik had died on impact; it was the life support that was keeping him alive. The doctors informed his mother that they had to switch off the machine and let him go. Nik was dead, and I had to tell the children. It was the hardest part because I did not understand it myself. So how was I going to make them understand? All the lights in my head went out. I was in a muffled world, switching between reality and what I thought was fiction. I was lost in the middle of nowhere, unable to find the connecting dots. I broke the news to the girls and tried to explain it so they would both understand. I knew the road ahead would be extremely difficult for all of us.

ACTUAL COLLISION PICTURES

Post spears windscreen in A47 accident

Nikolas Martins of New Parks, Boulevard, Leicester, was taken to Addenbrookes Hospital after the collision, which happened at 3:20pm at Thornhaugh close to its junction with Old Oundle Road.

He received serious injuries from a post which speared the windscreen of the BMW car he was travelling in.

The driver of the car, a 39-year-old woman from Leicester, was arrested on suspicion of drunk driving and has been bailed until May 6. The other occupants of the vehicle, two girls aged 11 and 6, suffered slight injuries and were taken to Peterborough City Hospital.

Man, 36, dies from injuries sustained in A47 crash when fence post speared windscreen

The BMW which crashed into fence along the A47 at Peterborough

Thursday, February 20, 2014
9:58 AM

A 36-year-old man who was speared by a post when a car left the road and collided with a fence on Sunday has died.

~ ~ ~

It was the 5th of January 2015. The day I dreaded had finally reached me, my criminal court case at Peterborough Crown Court. I hardly slept the night before. I was entering into an unknown zone where it was potentially hazardous. It had been almost a year since I lost my Nik and I still cried for him every day. It had been almost ten months since I was ordered to leave my home and my children. It had been three months since the final court order was granted to make Aunt Marjorie the official guardian to my children. A lot of bad things had happened and yet there was more to come, I had to face the judge who was sentencing me for the death of Nikolas Martins. I had prepared my children, on our last contact, for the possibility of imprisonment.

I spent the night before packing all my belongings into suitcases in case I was sent to prison. I had arranged with the social worker to pick the children up and take them to Nina's in the event that I did not return from court. Although all the professionals working with me at that time told me that prison was inevitable, I did not believe them. I still believed that what happened on the 16th of February 2014 was an act of God. Seven days before Nik was taken away, I made a powerful and emotional prayer to God, asking Him to intervene because the situation had reached boiling point. I asked God to end the misery for myself and for Nik. I never dreamt that He would end it with death, but was it a coincidence? I never prayed for Nik to die. I strongly believe that nobody dies before their time, and when it is your time, no matter where you are, death will find you. And what about all those times he talked about his own death and even said, *"Nicolette, you are going to be the death of me. I will die at 36?"* We had just celebrated his 36th birthday two weeks prior, on the 26th of January 2014.

I was advised by my probation officer that when people go to prison, they take a few clothes with them and anything else they might need for the period of incarceration. But because I did not believe that I would be sentenced to prison, I did not pack anything. However, I did withdraw £300 from the savings account, just in case. My 'just in case' was two out of a hundred chances. God did not let accidents like that happen just for show. There had to be a reason behind such a fatal accident with four people in the vehicle when three people walked out unscathed and only one died on the spot. He went on impact; he made no sound at all. It was over in a flash. I did not know the reason why God saved my children and me, but I did not believe that He saved us to prolong the pain. No, that was not the God of my understanding. It was not His style.

I arrived at the crown court just after nine-thirty am and went to the reception to sign in, only to be told that my case was scheduled for two o'clock that afternoon. I was gutted; I could have had some more sleep, but I did not want to be late, since I had it down for ten am. I was feeling tired, so I went to sit in the waiting area and decided to take a nap. I must have been really tired because when I opened my eyes and looked at the clock, it had gone after one pm. I went to the bathroom to freshen up and then went outside for a cigarette. Whilst outside, I saw my solicitor coming through. We walked back in together and took a seat where we were joined by the barrister who had also just walked in. They explained the procedure.

A few moments later, I saw four officers walk in with a woman and they sat adjacent to where we were. My heart missed a beat - and then started pounding: it was Nik's mother escorted by officials. I did not recognise the uniform that the officers wore. I had never seen it before. They wore smart black trousers and a blazer - with a white shirt - and a black cap. They had several medals on their blazers, so I figured they were important officials. I never did find out who these officials were or what their capacity was, but it did not stop me from wondering.

I did not know what to do. She was sitting with these officers and they were in deep conversation. I was not sure whether to approach her or not. I was not even sure if she had spotted me. His mother had aged since the last time I saw her at my house. She looked frail and sad; and it hit me that I was the cause of her turmoil. My solicitor advised me that it was best I did not approach them, so I remained seated and felt extremely uncomfortable. I went outside again for a cigarette. The emotions were running wild in my body. I had no one with me on that day. No friend, and no family. I was all alone faced with all these intimidating officials, including the barristers, solicitors, and the judge. I felt as though I was in a lion's den about to be devoured alive.

After briefing me, my solicitor and barrister left, and I remained seated on my own with Mummy seated just a few metres away. After a while I saw her get up and walk towards me, but her eyes were focused, not in my direction, but straight ahead. As she got closer my heart was hammering.

"Hello Mummy_," I said to her as she passed me. She did not answer and did not look at me. She passed me as if I were not there. I was hurt, but at the same time, I could understand why she did not want to have anything to do with me. I was the person responsible for the death of her beloved son. She was living with the loss and pain that I had caused her. She was headed for the toilet, so I made myself disappear before she returned, knowing she would have to pass me again. I wanted to make it less painful and awkward for her. I went outside for another fag, and when I came back, I sat in a chair where my view was blocked so she would not see me. I figured that I was a reminder of her anguish.

Just after two pm my name was called out for court 7. I was directed inside by an usher and was guided behind a glass room at the back of the court, which had a door that led downstairs. I was facing the judge and was guarded by a security officer on my right. On my far right sat Mummy and the four officers. I wanted the ground to open up and swallow me. The courtroom was occupied by me, the guard, Mummy and the four officers. There were also solicitors, my barrister, the prosecution and of course the court stenographer. Seeing Nik's mum was a shock, I was not expecting anyone to turn up. I guess she wanted to see for herself that I got the punishment I deserved.

ACTUAL JUDGE'S STATEMENT

"Nicolette Wallace, you've pleaded guilty at an early stage to this offence_____ and I do think that you have shown some awareness of the very serious offence you have committed, and I will give you full credit for your early plea, of course, and for that degree of recognition on your part.

"I am not going to say anything at all about your relationship with the man who died in this accident. I'm quite certain that there is more than one side to it but none of that really matters today. The fact is that he has been killed and that was due to your careless driving under the influence of alcohol, and so nothing that I'm going to say today or the sentence that I'm going to impose has anything to do with your past relationship in any way at all.

*"Your records show, as counsel has quite rightly acknowledged, a condition of **entrenched alcoholism** and it may well be that the level of alcohol in your blood at this time was in a sense an operating level and it may well be that you did not feel as drunk as you were__ You apparently negotiated about 35 miles and were not driving unduly fast, but you had really an appallingly high level of alcohol in your blood__*

"The serious nature of this offence really requires me to pass a significant custodial sentence; there's simply no way around that...

"I accept that the sentence that I'm bound to impose **will cause great hardship to you,** *but not only to you* **but to your children as well,** *particularly one daughter whom I am told is afflicted. All I can do in these circumstances is impose a sentence that I think is appropriate* **and as low as I can**, *given the fact that this man's death was caused while you were very much under the influence of alcohol* **although not driving too fast and probably guilty of only a moment or two of inattention."**

"In view of your previous record which features a previous matter in 2010 for excess alcohol and then subsequently driving whilst disqualified, I don't think that the starting point represents the appropriate sentence. On the other hand, given the mitigation that has been put before me, **nor do I think it would be likely to increase it unduly much.** *Having taken all that into account, the sentence of the Court, is slightly longer than four-and-a-half years. I hereby sentence you to fifty-six months imprisonment where you will serve half of your sentence incarcerated and the other half on license. I also ban you from driving any motor vehicle for a period of five years."*

My heart sank, everything around me was crumbling before my eyes. I cried in disbelief. I avoided looking in the direction where Mummy and the officers were seated. In the box room behind the glass, the security guard who was standing beside me, pointed towards the door behind us. He led me downstairs to the reception where there was a lot of paperwork to fill in. Everything was happening in slow motion; I could see people's lips moving but all I could hear were sounds. Everyone was walking in slow motion; my head was spinning.

"I'm going to prison. Jail? It can't be. No way, how come? My mind kept talking. The news had not sunk in yet. After filling out a bunch of forms I was led down the corridor and into one of the cells. The sound of the steel door shutting and keys turning brought me back to life for a few seconds. The room was tiny and filthy with a long wooden bench running along from one end to another. The walls full of graffiti, words that had been written by previous occupiers before me.

MARK WAS HERE 13/06/13.   Fuck the justice system. *Judge McIntosh, you stink*, were some of the writings. The wall was covered in meaningless messages. It was as if everyone who had been in that cell had left a signature. Maybe if I had a writing instrument, I might have left mine. The writing on the wall kept me entertained for a little while, and then it all came back to me.

I was going to jail. I, Nicolette Wallace, was going to prison. For the next two-and-a-half years, jail would be my home and my life. My children... and with that thought, I broke down. I would not survive without my children for that long. I felt a deep, sharp pain in my chest and the warmness of my tears rolling down my cheeks. I sobbed uncontrollably. The reality was kicking in and my mind was overloading. I was having a panic attack. I stood up from the bench and started pacing up and down from wall to wall. I could feel the physical pain of my heart beating fast and I was having trouble breathing.

"C'mon Nic breathe," I told myself. I took deep breaths in and out as my pace increased. The room was getting smaller and smaller and my brain felt as if it were about to explode. I needed some air. Just then I heard the rattling of keys. The steel door was flung open.

"Miss Wallace, your solicitor is here to see you, follow me."

I was led to a room just as small as the cell I was in. My solicitor and barrister were seated on the other side of the desk, and there was an empty chair near the entrance. The look on both their faces confirmed my fears: it was not a nightmare; no, I *was* going to jail. It was a done deal. There was nothing else they could do for me. They explained that I was going to be transported to HMP Peterborough which was the local jail. There, I would be serving twenty-eight months; half of the sentence - and would serve the rest in the community on license. It was the 6th of January 2015, and would be released from jail on the 6th of May 2017.

"I can't do it!" I cried; my chest felt heavy from the pain. If pain alone could kill, I would have died that day in that tiny office. When they were done with me, I was led to another room by the same security guard. He took my bag and emptied its contents onto the desk. He opened the envelope which contained my money and counted it.

"£300.00, okay sign here please to confirm the amount. I am going to take this off you for now and everything else you've got in your bag, it will all be given back to you when you arrive at your destination." I signed more paperwork, and then he placed all my belongings in a plastic bag and sealed it. I was taken back to the cell awaiting transportation.

"No please don't put me back there! I am having panic attacks_" the words did not come out. I was talking within myself. I was too weak and very muddled. I was back in the cell with my mind going insane. The thought of my children broke my heart into a million pieces. I had to keep moving my body to slow down my mind which was in a whirlwind. I kept reassuring myself and walking around the room. Space was limited, but I realised that I had to get used to it. It was going to be my life for the next two-and-a-half years. *It is what it is.*

After what seemed like a lifetime the steel door was unlocked again, and two officers were standing outside.

"You ready Miss Wallace? Your transport is here," said one of them, a chubby man with a balding head, probably in his mid-fifties. The other one was a tall, slim, dark-haired officer, about 6ft tall. I placed him in his late twenties or early thirties. I was handcuffed to the chubby chap who accompanied me out of the building and on to a white van waiting in the parking area at the back of the court. I was put into a cubicle the size of a public telephone booth. It had a steel bench and was just enough to fit one seated person, with no room to spread out your legs. Once inside, the officer uncuffed me and shut the door, and I heard the keys turning. I was locked in this little cubicle they called the 'sweatbox' with no windows and no fresh air. I could see the view outside, but from outside no one could see the view inside. I supposed it was to protect the prisoners.

By then, I was exhausted and had lost track of time, but it was dark outside, so I knew it was late in the day. I closed my eyes as the van made its way to my new home. My mind was battling with all sorts of thoughts. I was petrified. I tried to picture what jail would be like, I had watched many films about prison, and they were not pleasant.

> "I am going to be beaten and sexually abused. Oh God, please get me out of this situation. You are a God of miracles, work your magic and get me out of here. Please, God, I am begging you. I cannot go to jail. I won't survive."

I could not control the tears, the pain in my chest was excruciating.

The van came to a halt, and I heard voices. We waited there for over ten minutes before it started moving again. After a few yards, it stopped again and moments later my door was unlocked. I was led inside to the reception area. I filled out a few forms then was directed to the holding area. There were seven other women in there, each face telling a different story. It was quiet. No one seemed to want to engage in conversation. Some were seated on the sofas and others were pacing up and down, cursing.

"Wallace!" I heard a female voice shouting. I left the holding area and went to the reception desk; there was more paperwork before I was led to the office where my photograph was taken. I looked a right mess from the tiredness and the crying. I was in jail. *"I am in jail."* The more I said it to myself, the more it did not seem real. I had to wake up from the nightmare. Everything was a blur. I heard voices, doors shutting, keys jingling and saw a lot of prison guards moving. My mind was trying to make sense of what was going on around me, but it was shutting down. I was then directed to the nurse who asked about my health and then was tested for drugs and alcohol. From there, I was taken to another room where I was strip-searched. How humiliating it was, to take off my clothes in front of total strangers. I put my clothes back on and was led to yet another office.

"Here is a list of our emergency canteen, tick the things you need for now until our next canteen order which is done every Thursday. Do you smoke?"

"Yes" I answered. As a matter of fact, I had been dying for a fag, but I was not allowed any during the whole booking process. I ticked some toiletries, tea bags, juice and three packs of amber leaf tobacco. There was a £15 limit for everybody. The money would be paid back weekly from wages. I was given some clothes, underwear, nightie, plimsolls and toiletries. The cup, plate, and bowl were all in blue plastic. I then returned to the holding area. The situation was becoming too overwhelming for me, so I ran to the reception toilets and broke down.

"Are you okay?" I heard a voice just outside the compartment I was in. I opened the door and saw a black girl of medium build, about 5ft 7 who had her weave in a ponytail tied at the back with a middle parting in the front. "Girl you need to be strong, there's no need to be crying. You are here now, so you have to deal with the situation as it is. You gotta be strong to survive in here."

I cried some more. I could not speak; I could just nod to her. There was now twelve of us in the holding cell and only two of us were black. I was so exhausted. All I wanted were to rest my body. Just after eleven pm every one of us prisoners had been booked in and were now being escorted to the induction wing. A lot of bar gates were being locked and unlocked every few steps. We were all allocated to our cells, and that is when I found out that it was a double cell. I had to share with another person.

"Oh no please, I cannot share with anybody else. I need to be alone, please". I begged the male officer.

"Sorry love, this is what you are getting, you two will be sharing this cell." He was referring to the black girl who had consoled me earlier in reception toilets. *Oh no!*

The cell consisted of a double-decker steel bed, with a thin blue plastic mattress. A desk and an open wardrobe about half a metre wide with shelves. It was about three metres high. Just behind the wardrobe was the toilet. It was situated next to the door, with no privacy. There was also a sink next to it. I looked into the mirror above the sink and saw myself. *"No, it's not a dream, you really are, in prison. You are in jail and this is going to be your home for the next two-and-a-half years."*

Brevita, my cellmate, took the bottom bunk whilst I climbed up the top. I looked around me, trying to put the pieces together. The bits that my mind was missing. Within a few minutes, my pillow was soaking wet. I was crying silently because I did not want Brevita to hear me. I wanted to bellow out loud so that I could release the tension in my heart and soul, but I could not, the situation did not permit me. The sound of the steel door being bolted, almost made me jump out of my skin. I heard more bolting and the sound of keys jingling.

"LIGHTS OUT!" The officer shouted. Everything went quiet. That was my first night of the 852 to come.

EPILOGUE

Domestic abuse is real and domestic violence is happening. Many might ask why I stayed in an abusive relationship for so long. Some might even ask how I fell in love with someone who was volatile towards me, but, unfortunately, I do not have the answers to those questions. I do not have valid reasons, nor do I have meaningful explanations. One can never know a situation in its entirety until one walks the path. You can never know how much the shoe hurts until you put it on.

This is only a chapter of a series about the domestic abuse I have experienced. Before meeting with Nikolas Martins, my life had already been through a spiral of such events. The chapter before this talks in detail about the abuse that went on in my marriage. Ten years of the abuse I received from the father of my children. This is described in the title: *IT IS WHAT IT IS: 'Living in Sin'*.

According to the national statistics data, 2.3 million women experienced domestic abuse in the year ending March 2020. These figures are not even up to date because there are millions more who are experiencing domestic violence but are suffering in silence. Many incidents go unreported because the victims live in fear or have felt that they have been let down by the system. They see no point in calling the authorities, especially if it will get them into more trouble.

According to national statistical data, "**Domestic abuse is often a hidden crime that is not reported to the police.**

Therefore, data held by the police can only provide a partial picture of the actual level of domestic abuse experienced. Many cases will not enter the criminal justice process, as they are not reported to the police."

I accept that I had a part to play; there was a chance I could have walked away in the very beginning when the red flag started flashing. I made an error, and my biggest mistake was that I forgave, and I kept forgiving and making excuses. In the process, I destroyed people's lives, most hurtful of all: my children's.

According to the general principle of the practice directions 12J, **"Domestic abuse is harmful to children, and/or puts children at risk of harm, whether they are subjected to domestic abuse, or witness one of their parents being violent or abusive to the other parent or live in a home in which domestic abuse is perpetrated (even if the child is too young to be conscious of the behaviour). Children may suffer direct physical, psychological and/or emotional harm from living with domestic abuse and may also suffer harm indirectly where the domestic abuse impairs the parenting capacity of either or both of their parents."**

My children have suffered a developmental ailment caused by the trauma. Knowing all these facts breaks my heart, and at times I am angry with myself for allowing it to happen. But looking back, I see how weak I was, how vulnerable and how I was easy prey. I was empty inside. The kind of hollowness that left me abandoned and deserted in the middle of nowhere, longing for human contact. For understanding, care, love and affection. I was blinded, and then I lost track.

When social services first got involved in my children's lives, I did my best to work with them. I reported incidents as they happened; I showed them my phone and my emails to prove my contact with Nik. They would get a statement from me, but once it was on paper, it had a different meaning, painting the worst scenario. Words were twisted and actions manipulated. They would often have reports stating that I was spotted in the city centre with Nik just because I was seen walking with a male. I tried to defend myself, but I was dealing with six to eight powerful professionals at a time. I felt intimidated and threatened, and I lost my voice. In the end, I let them write what they wanted because I no longer had the strength to fight.

They stated that I was putting my needs first before my own children, but I requested on many occasions for assistance to move from the address, to be moved far from Nik's reach. All that was never considered; their advice and orders were, *"Do not open the door for him"*. When I obeyed the rule, he would retaliate by breaking my windows—all reported to the police. I ended up not trusting anyone and chose to suffer in silence. By doing so, I isolated myself from friends and family until it was just me, my children and our perpetrator.

My journey does not end here; there were still more challenges ahead of me. The next title: ***IT IS WHAT IT IS 'A Mother Behind Bars',*** details my journey through the two-and-a-half years I stayed behind bars at Peterborough Prison—its challenges, experiences, lessons, and more trouble ahead.

Too many mothers are in prison, too many children are in foster care due to domestic violence. If the system can work well internally and with victims, earn their trust and not fear, this situation might change. Intervention is needed, but to intervene with a threat of 'removing the children' is enough to frighten any mother wanting to seek help.

ABOUT THE AUTHOR

KikiDee 'KiDe' Kwetemu Watson, originally from Malawi, was born in Zimbabwe in 1974. She is the first child of a family of four, consisting of two girls and two boys. KikiDee is a legal secretary by profession and a former actress in Zimbabwe.

KikiDee moved to the United Kingdom in 1998 and now lives there permanently.

She is the mother of two beautiful girls, and she considers herself greatly blessed to be their mother. She is currently writing her book series. She also enjoys writing poetry which she hopes to publish someday.

Follow KikiDee on social media:

Email: kikidee0729@yahoo.co.uk

Website: http://www.kidekikidee.simplesite.com

Facebook: @KikiDee 'KiDe' Kwetemu Watson

Twitter: @kide75663153

LinkedIN: Kikidee Watson